A Tour Guide's
Sonoma Wine Country

Ralph & Lahni DeAmicis

Cuore Libre Publishing
Napa California

A Tour Guide's Sonoma Wine Country
Ralph & Lahni DeAmicis

Published by
Cuore Libre Publishing
Napa, California

To Order Copies Phone visit
www.WineCountryAtWork.com

Copyright © 2021 by Ralph & Lahni DeAmicis
Photos: Lahni DeAmicis
Maps: Ralph DeAmicis
ISBN 978-1-931163-73-6

Disclaimer: We create these books through extensive research that includes having visited many of these wineries multiple times. But we make no guarantees for the accuracy of the information included herein, and accept no responsibility for any losses or inconvenience you may suffer from using this product. Important: Our advice is intended to help you stay safe while you enjoy the region, but mixing alcohol and driving is a risky endeavor. We suggest that you approach it cautiously by having a designated or professional driver. We want you to have a fun time in Wine Country and come back and visit again and again.

Ralph & Lahni DeAmicis

Contents

Maps Directory 4
Introduction to the Tour Guide's Perspective 5
Chapter One: Creating a Day Trip Strategy 7
Chapter Two: Visiting from San Francisco 13
Chapter Three: Navigating Wine Country Safely 19
Chapter Four: Choosing Wineries Wisely 23
Chapter Five: Our Best Tasting Room Tips 27
Chapter Six: Ralph's ABC's for Tasting Wine 31
Chapter Seven: Navigating Sonoma 37
Chapter Eight: The Sonoma Valley 43
Chapter Nine: Northern Sonoma & Healdsburg 47
Chapter Ten: The Russian River Valley 51
Chapter Eleven: The Dry Creek Valley 55
Chapter Twelve: The Alexander Valley 61
Answer A: You Gotta Eat! 65
Answer B: Clothing, Wine Country Casual 69
Answer C: Find the Grapes You Love 73
Answer D: Transportation 77
Answer E: The Art & Science of Winemaking 81
Answer F: Taste Buds & Tasting Notes 85
Answer G: Tasting Fees, Wine Clubs & Shipping 87
Using the Directory & Maps 91
Winery Directory 95
About the Authors 174
Bonus Chapter - Visiting with Children 175
Two Bonus Tales from 'Wine Country in Shorts' 183
The Directory Maps 192 - 199
Catalog 200

Map Directory

Page 12: Travel Times from San Francisco

Page 18: Sonoma and Napa County Overview

Page 22: Sonoma American Viticulture Areas

Page 36: Sonoma & Napa Main Roads

Page 42: The Sonoma Valley Overview

Page 60: Northern Sonoma Overview

Page 90: Overview of the Southern Wine Country

Page 192 Map A: The Sonoma Plaza

Page 193 Map B: First Stops Coming from the South

Page 194 Map C: Los Carneros Wineries in Two Counties

Page 195 Map D: Sonoma Valley Wineries

Page 196 Map E: The Russian River Valley Wineries

Page 197 Map F: Dry Creek Valley Wineries

Page 198 Map G: Alexander Valley Wineries

Page 199 Map H: Downtown Healsburg

Introduction to the Tour Guide's Perspective

This book is written from the perspective of two tour guides, a profession that views the region from two sides. We see our guests' wide-eyed, slightly inebriated enjoyment of the great wines and remarkable experiences, and we also see how much work our winery neighbors put into creating them. It is a synergistic relationship, which is why this region continues to evolve and so have our books. Our intention is to help you enjoy your time in Wine Country so we base our recommendations on our many clients' experiences and comments over the years.

Sonoma is a place of great beauty, mystery and fertility, and her most remarkable feature is her diversity. She is like a beautiful woman with many skills and talents, yet she still tends the garden, prepares the food and sings the songs of her ancestors. When you are standing on the banks of the Russian River, surrounded by a fairy ring of giant redwood trees stretching from deep in the earth up to the heavens, it is reassuring to realize that there is that much beauty in the world. When you breathe in the salt spray of the rolling Pacific Ocean, standing on the spectacular Sonoma coastline, it is inspiring. When you sit on a patio sipping a glass of wine in one of Sonoma's abundantly fertile valleys, enjoying the view of the vines, it is intoxicating on more than just the physical level. When you visit Sonoma, you are experiencing the deep beauty of the divine feminine, so it's no wonder that it feels so special!

While you might think that wine tourism is Sonoma's bread and butter, winemaking is the bigger business and Sonoma is a surprisingly big player on the global stage. But because everything grows so well here, Sonoma has been producing a wide variety of excellent agricultural products since the mid 1800's, even though wine has become the biggest moneymaker. Sonoma has always been blessed with tourists, first for the hot springs, then for the beaches, camping and rafting. But it was wine tourism that brought so many great restaurants here, sparking the farm to table movement, because it is the easiest way for the local chefs to work their magic. For the folks that work in the vineyards and wineries, the idea that people want to see how the grapes are turned into wine is delightful, since they are also enthusiasts, which is what makes them wonderful hosts, they hope you will enjoy this place as much as they do.

A note about the design of this book. The first six chapters share helpful information about the North Bay Wine Country. The next six chapters are about exploring Sonoma. The following seven 'Answers' are responses to the 'questions' that we have most often heard from clients.

Following that is the Winery Directory: Fair warning, the directory is neither comprehensive nor guaranteed accurate, because wineries are notoriously bad at informing tour book authors about their many changes. Check their websites before you visit because many Sonoma wineries now require appointments. *After the directory are three bonus chapters.*

Then come the maps. We make them as accurate and readable as possible, but they are primarily intended as overviews of Sonoma's location and its grape growing areas. While GPS mostly works well, many wineries often post more specific directions on their websites, so use those.

On AmicisTours.com there are numerous videos and full TV episodes from our show 'Wine Country at Work' that you might find illuminating. So good luck navigating Sonoma and we hope that our book leads you to delightful experiences and diversions.

Chapter One: Creating a Day Trip Strategy

Every wine tour needs a great strategy to take the best advantage of the day. Over the course of thousands of tours with clients, we've had the opportunity to see what works, and what doesn't. Here are some of our best tips! The first step is to start early! If drinking wine in the morning seems excessive, remember, you are in a 'tasting' room, not a 'drinking' room. You are there to evaluate and enjoy the wines, not aiming to get a buzz on. There is a big difference between wine tasting and bar hopping!

Winery tasting rooms are generally open from 10am to 5pm. So, if you arrive early the staff is still fresh. Many people working in the tasting rooms routinely taste each bottle to make sure the wine is okay, and the alcohol adds up. By the latter part of the day, they can get pretty loose, and by the end of the day they are also tired. You want them pouring for you when they are sharp and happy to answer questions.

Also, if it is an open tasting room with other clients around, it can get noisy and a little messy later in the day, and the service can be a bit iffy. The best times to taste are between 10am and 3pm. That doesn't mean people don't frequently go to 5pm and bit more, if they can manage it. For the wineries, sometimes those late day tastings, when guests are feeling no pain, can be good sales opportunities. But, from your side of the tasting bar, if you want to avoid buying more wine than you intended, avoid stretching the day.

As tour drivers, we believe strongly in the good sense of hiring someone to drive for you, rather than taking the chance of drinking and driving with the inherent physical and legal risks that entails. However, we know from experience that many people drive themselves, and if care and moderation are taken, it can be done safely. We explain how to do that in the next chapter. Also, even when you hire a driver, you may want to plan the tour yourself, especially if the person driving is not an expert on the wine region. Transportation is the largest employer of men in America, so you can figure that a certain percentage live by their GPS and are clueless about the winding, steep canyon roads that make up wine country. Local tour guides rarely depend on GPS because the limited number of towers combined with the steep hills makes it undependable. When you plan your day the first question is whether or not you are driving yourself, because those suggest two differnt strategies.

When driving yourself, plan the longest leg of the trip for the beginning of the day, when you have no alcohol in your system. Head to the farthest winery first, and then plan that each subsequent leg of the trip will bring you closer to your starting point. Plan to have lunch after the first winery at a location on the route between the first and the second winery. Don't rush lunch, but do not let it take more than an hour. When driving yourself visiting two wineries, one before and one after a gracious lunch, is about right. For the winery after lunch, choose one that is as close to where you are staying as possible.

That doesn't mean it needs to be next to your hotel, although if there was a spectacular tasting room walking distance, that would be fine. In fact, some of the downtown wineries these days are excellent for walk-about tastings. In any case your ride back from the final winery, when you are tired and maybe a little tipsy, shouldn't be more than about ten to fifteen minutes.

Two wineries in a day with a lunch in between is safe, if the person driving exercises moderation, eats plenty of protein and fat and drinks enough water: one ounce for each ounce of wine.

If someone is driving who is not drinking, you can plan a little differently and visit more wineries. The first winery will be closer to your starting point. Choose a winery where the wines will be light in flavor and alcohol, so your palate can warm up and not become immediately saturated. With a designated driver you can go to two wineries before lunch.

The second winery should be the farthest from your starting point. That way you are relaxed by the wine and in a good mood for the ride between the first and the second winery. The next should feature 'bigger wines', with fuller flavors, which means fewer white wines and more reds (unless you don't like red wine). After the second tasting, enjoy a nice lunch, once again, high in protein and fat and low in simple carbohydrates.

Warning!!! Never go to more than two tastings without eating! Often after the second winery you are feeling like you have superpowers, and you are up for another tasting adventure. Don't fall for that! If you do not get enough protein and fat into your system, your blood sugar will plummet, and you'll need a nap.

After lunch, the next winery should be closer to your starting point. Some tours lend themselves to a fourth winery. It depends on the types of wines you're drinking. The bigger, more expensive wines have higher alcohol and require longer tastings to allow them to open. The sparkling wines, whites and light reds are shorter sessions. If you add a fourth winery it should be the closet to your starting point. What you want to avoid is a long drive back to your lodging when you are tired. At the end of the day, after a bunch of wine and sun, you will need a nap. The question is, do you want to take that nap in the car or beside the pool?

Hint: About that fourth winery. Having big red wines on top of big reds can so saturate the palate that it is hard to tell them apart, so having a prestigious red wine late in the day is often a waste of time and tasting endurance. Ideally, plan to visit those wineries immediately before and after lunch.

At the first winery your palate is still waking up and by the fourth winery your palate is saturated, and your nervous system is sedated, so it's hard to enjoy the flavors. The best wines for late in the day are sparkling wines, because their high acid levels and of course, the bubbles, clean the palate and bring a touch of delight and celebration to the end of the day.

Wineries have increasingly moved to seated tastings that require 90 minutes. Allow for 20 minutes between each stop and an hour for lunch, so three wineries take 5 to 7 hours and four wineries take 7 to 8 hours. When there were more 30-45 minute walk-in bar tastings, we could bring our guests to 5 wineries in 6 to 7 hours, but those are less common today.

It is a Matter of Timing

Early in the day, the staff tends to pour smaller samples, but as the day goes on the samples expand a bit so after 3pm, all bets are off, and you'd better watch out. As the day passes it is increasingly important to drink enough water. Late in the day most people forget. As a guide, I am continually handing guests cold bottles of spring water. If the tasting room host knows you have a professional driver, they will often pour more wine because they're not concerned about you driving into a ditch. They will also pour better wines because they know that 'buyers' often hire drivers.

This is important because the winery staff works by commission and they know that the more wine they pour the more they sell. They pour more during the seated tastings, which give guests enough time to appreciate the wines and engage with the host, which is a big part of sales. Not surprisingly, seated tasting sales are significantly higher than those at a bar, which is why bar tastings are disappearing. Wineries are good places to buy wine because they keep their best bottles for their visitors.

Watch out, occasionally hosts get out of control and take those big pours to extremes. First, that's dangerous because drunks get behind the wheel, or fall on their face. Second, excessive alcohol is toxic, and the guests suffer the next day. Finally, inhibitions dissolve and visitors can find a nasty charge on their credit card bill, for wines they barely remember tasting or buying! That is why we suggest not stretching the day! It is also why we recommend using the 'dump buckets'.

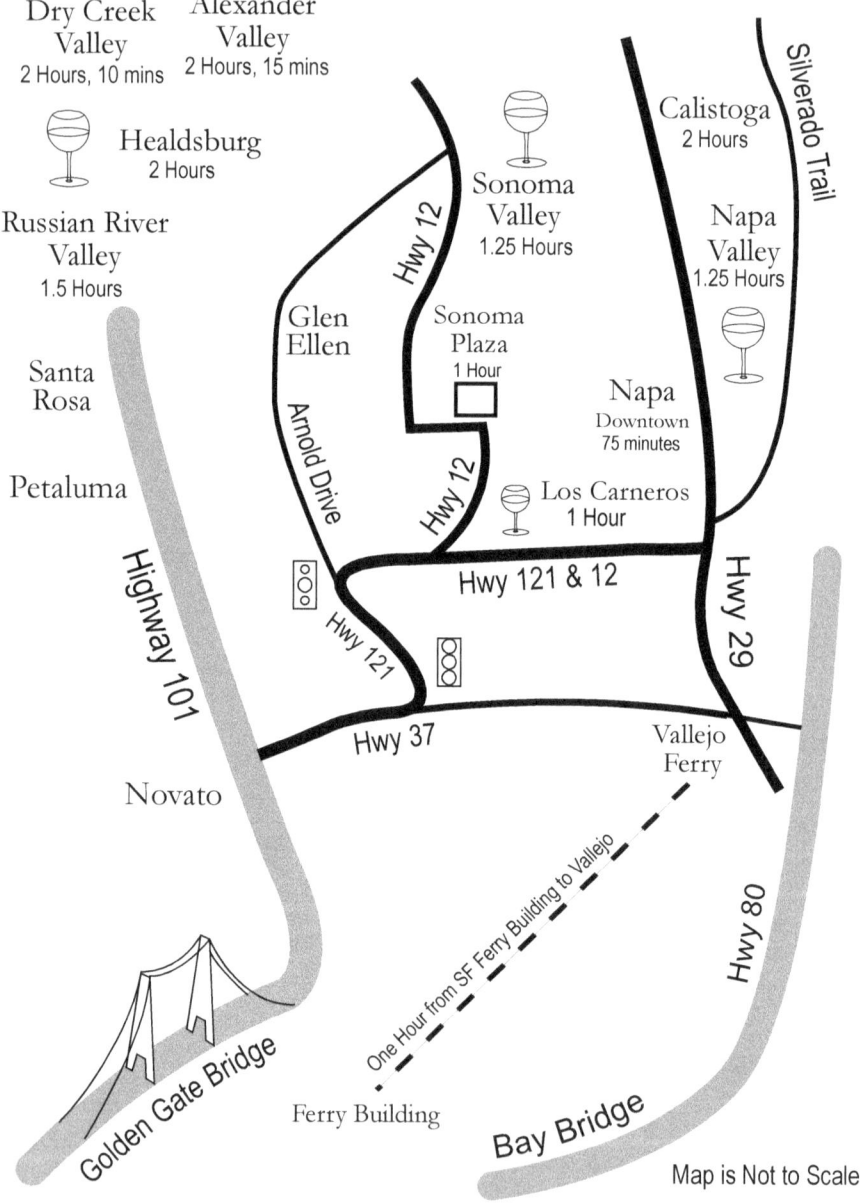

Chapter Two: Visiting from San Francisco

Californian's love this region and about sixty percent of the visitors come from the Bay Area. On top of that, people visit from all over the world and a good number of them drive up from San Francisco, one of the world's most popular tourist destinations. Part of the enticement is the convenience; the first Sonoma vineyards are thirty minutes north of the Golden Gate Bridge (GG). Downtown Sonoma and Napa are another half hour, so day tripping to the wineries is easy to do. The biggest strategic hurdles are avoiding traffic and managing your alcohol consumption.

Sonoma County is three times larger than Napa County and the wine regions are spread out, so our Sonoma recommendation from SF is to visit downtown Sonoma and the Valley of the Moon immediately north, which is filled with great wineries. Our Napa suggestion is to visit the wineries of Los Carneros, and the valley between the city of Napa and the town of Rutherford.

From San Francisco, the beautiful route is north on Highway 101, over the Golden Gate Bridge to Route 37 East and then Highway 121 North. It is less stressful and trafficked than the massive Bay Bridge and the congested East Bay highways. There are more places to stop for coffee, restaurants, vistas, bathrooms, and interesting side trips, like Sausalito and Muir Woods. In

San Francisco, Hwy 101 travels along Van Ness Avenue before turning onto Lombard Street where it skirts the historic military base called the Presidio and crosses the GG bridge. From there, you will enjoy spectacular views of Alcatraz, Angel Island (the Ellis Island of the West), the Marin Headlands to the west and the Golden Gate pass. On the north landing of the bridge is a breezy Vista Point. At the top of the hill is the Robin Williams Tunnel, with its rainbow border. After the tunnel, Sausalito is on the right with their famous houseboats. We suggest making a separate side trip to Sausalito, Tiburon (a smaller, upscale Sausalito), the Marin Headlands with its views, Rodeo Beach and Muir Woods for the towering redwoods.

Both Tiburon and Sausalito can be reached from SF by ferries. Combining any of these with a Wine Country trip can result in an exhausting day. You can also reach Napa, via Vallejo, by boat from the SF Ferry Building. You will need to arrange with a tour company to pick you up at the Vallejo Terminal.

Sonoma and Napa Counties are located at the north edge of the bay, so driving north on Hwy 101, you will see water on your right. There are actually two bays; San Francisco Bay abeam the GG Bridge, and farther north, San Pablo Bay, which borders Sonoma and Napa. Route 37 travels east from 101 along the top of the bay through Sonoma, Napa, and Vallejo, to Hwy 80. When you cross the bridge over the Petaluma River into Sonoma, the rolling hills are shared by cattle and vines.

Landmarks: Look for the Sonoma Racetrack sign on the left side, with its turbocharged cow on top. At that traffic light, turn left onto Highway 121. This is the cool, windy Los Carneros AVA (American Viticulture Area) the only one that spans Sonoma and Napa, along the northern edge of the Bay. This region favors Chardonnay and Pinot Noir and it includes several sparkling wine producers. There are a group of reasonably priced, popular wineries along this part of the road that make good first stops.

You will see numerous Shepherds' Crooks topped with a Bell on the way to downtown Sonoma, with the final one standing in front of the Mission on the historic Plaza. This marks the route as part of El Camino Real, or the Royal Highway from the time when California was part of Spain and later Mexico.

Some First Stop Options

The first winery you see is Ram's Gate. They do a seated tasting by appointment, with nice views of Los Carneros and the wetlands. Many of these 'first stop' wineries do not normally require appointments but check online. Viansa's hilltop tasting and deli is popular with buses and corporate groups. Next comes Jacuzzi which shares its building with the Olive Press. Across the road is Cline, offering tastings of a wide selection of varietals. Late in the day these wineries are packed by people making one last stop as they head south. *See the 'First Stop' map B on page 193.*

A little farther on is the expansive Estate of Gloria Ferrer, sparkling wines in an elegant, Spanish style tasting room and patio, with lovely views. Across the road is a complex called Cornerstone Gardens, with several tasting rooms, shops, galleries, and a deli in case you forgot breakfast. Nearby are four small wineries: Anaba, popular with the little tour buses, Schug, well known for its Pinots, the wonderful Robledo family with great wines with good prices, Roche, long-time growers with a beautiful new winery and hospitality complex.

Going to Downtown Sonoma and the Sonoma Valley

At the first blinking traffic light, bear right following Highway 121. At the next traffic light, if you turn left onto Highway 12 North, that will bring you to Sonoma's historic Plaza. It is the largest plaza in California and it has plenty of restaurants, stores, galleries, a couple of museums, two playgrounds and an abundance of winery tasting rooms. This a good place for lunch and a stroll. At the Plaza, Highway 12 North turns left and winds through the little town into the heart of the 15-mile-long 'Valley of the Moon'.

Going to Napa

Napa is to the east of Sonoma, so instead of going north on Highway 12, continue east on Highway 121, Carneros Highway. In about ten minutes you will come to the traffic light at the T intersection with Hwy 29. On the way you will see numerous Los Carneros wineries; Nicholson Ranch (the last winery in Sonoma), Napa's Domaine Carneros (a French style chateau with sparkling wines), Cuvaison, Madonna Estate and Hyde.

In the hills to the north and south of the highway are other wineries, also specializing in Chardonnay and Pinot Noir; Donum, Calmére, Artesa, Truchard, Bouchaine, Saintsbury and Etude. At Hwy 29 turn left (north) towards the city of Napa and the Valley beyond.

The First Street exit goes to downtown Napa, a popular mix of tasting rooms, restaurants, stores, theaters, and hotels. Just across the Napa River is the popular Oxbow Artisans Market and the downtown campus of the Culinary Institute of America known locally as the CIA, which is very different from the one in Washington DC.

Ten minutes north of downtown on Hwy 29 is the beginning of the valley with its string of small, charming towns, starting with Yountville, Oakville (tiny), Rutherford (almost as tiny), St. Helena and Calistoga. The biggest concentration of wineries is from Yountville to St. Helena. From downtown Napa to the top of the valley takes 45 minutes.

About the Bay Bridge

We do not recommend this route because this is the busiest bridge in the Bay Area. The only time we take it is coming from SF to Napa early on a Sunday morning. By Sunday afternoons it is congested again. Hwy 80, the route that passes over the Bay Bridge is a huge road that passes through endless commercial and industrial areas, with rarely an enticing or convenient place to stop. While GPS says the mileage is shorter, the driving is longer, or at least it seems that way.

Timing the Traffic

If you are coming to wine country from the city during the week the traffic normally favors you because the rush hour cars are heading south when you are heading north. At the end of the day that reverses, so once again the traffic will be lighter heading back into the city. But, because there is a big bay in the middle of the 'Bay Area', you may encounter heavy cross-county traffic, so the routes we suggest are designed to avoid that.

One of the most troublesome Wine Country weekend traffic jams is in the afternoon on Carneros Hwy, Hwy 121, heading west, away from Napa and towards Route 37. That is because so many visitors are heading across Sonoma to get back to Marin and San Francisco. Leaving a bit earlier will allow you to avoid that. However, if you are coming from the Sonoma Valley, you can avoid that by taking Arnold Avenue south to Hwy 121. In fact, later in the day, those alternate routes, Arnold Avenue in Sonoma Valley and the Silverado Trail in Napa, can save you from sitting in traffic.

Sonoma and Napa County Overview

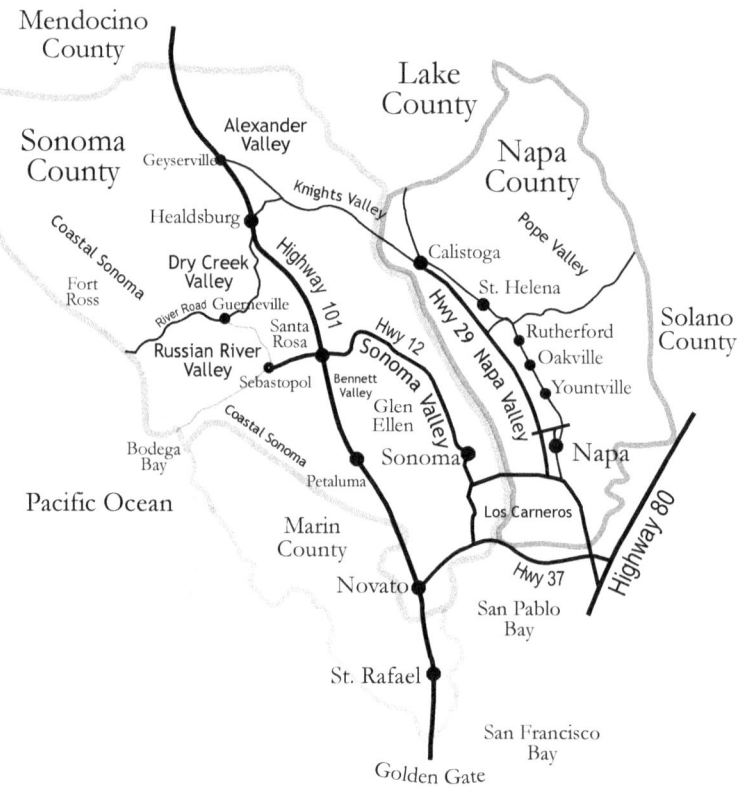

Chapter Three: Navigating Wine Country Safely

Wine Country tour book authors deal with a unique challenge; we are advising our readers about where to go, while realizing that they very possibly will be driving under the influence of alcohol. Not only that, but many of the people they will be sharing the roads with will be drinking and driving too. Drunk driving is so prevalent in this region that it has twice California's average of DUI's. When you combine that diminished capacity with narrow, winding, poorly marked and unlit country roads, Wine Country can be a dangerous place to get around. So, this chapter is about how to manage that as safely and successfully as possible. Like so many of life's pleasurable experiences, wine tasting is a favorite activity for couples. The first way that a couple can manage the total amount of alcohol they consume is by sharing a tasting. It is both practical and romantic, because, as you hand the glass back and forth, exchanging opinions and gazing into each other's eyes, you learn about each other's preferences and delights. That's the nature of romance and no one in Wine Country objects to that.

Winery regulations discourage drunkenness by telling wineries to pour one-ounce samples. That is a great plan, until a winery pours eight wines, which we have seen them do. A glass of wine in a restaurant is normally four to five ounces, so that is like having two glasses of wine. That's okay if that is the only winery you are visiting that day. However, wineries have increasingly moved to seated tastings behind closed doors, where they may pour fewer wines in a side by side arrangement, with larger amounts of wine in each glass. Of course, you don't have to drink all the wine, but when they are that delicious, leaving them un-drunk takes real discipline, which is not something people normally exhibit on vacation, especially when there is alcohol involved.

> *This is where sharing a tasting between a couple makes sense. They are often pouring more than enough for two people to sample.*

Additionally, male and female tasters have a physiological difference in their alcohol tolerance. That's because men make more of an enzyme that breaks down alcohol than women. As the tastings progress, women normally want to stop tasting sooner. When you share tastings, the woman doesn't feel like she is wasting wine if she leaves some in the glass, because the guy will probably finish it up, helpful fellow that he is. Because your total consumption is less, you can visit more wineries. As a bonus, you will probably remember which wineries you visited when you wake up in the morning. Admittedly some women have a higher alcohol tolerance, due to a longer history with alcohol. If they have normally drunk spirits, the more dilute alcohol in wine will have less of an effect. So, we are not saying that you must share tastings, we are saying that if you want to enjoy more wineries, this may be a great strategy.

If you feel uncomfortable saying that you want to share one tasting, use this tactic. Tell them that one of you doesn't drink, or at least not much. They are not going to monitor how much you share! Usually they will only charge you for one tasting, which is a nice savings since tasting fees have escalated over the years. And the free tasting is a thing of the past! The only time when this doesn't work is for tastings that include a tour or food pairing. In those situations, plan on paying full price for both people and everyone gets a glass. The side by side tastings are especially good for the bigger red wines that need time to open. There is no need for a dump bucket because the excess wine can remain in the glass and continue to evolve. If they do want to pour a second wine into one of the glasses, do not feel bad about pouring out a wine that doesn't appeal to you, or is just more than you want to drink. The hosts are not insulted by that sign of maturity. If you don't see a dump bucket handy, ask the staff for one. If the tasting only uses one glass, which is more common at bar tastings, make sure there is a dump bucket handy.

Here is a Another Less Popular Strategy

You can spit the wine out, which is what the professionals do at tastings. That works because your sensory experience of the wine happens in the nose and in the front half of the mouth. The bitter and sour flavors are tasted at the back of the mouth, but wines typically don't include those. So, you don't have to swallow the wine, with its alcohol, to analyze its flavors. Professionals also know that, thanks to the alcohol, after two or three sips, it all starts to taste good, which is a disadvantage when a pro is evaluating a wine.

There are three problems with spitting. First, you don't get the good feelings that come from the alcohol. Yes, we know that is the point, but that relaxed glow is part of what make a wine country trip fun. Second, spitting into a dump bucket is yucky for the people around you. Wine making is a messy business, so professionals are accustomed to this, but most tourists are not. Rather than spitting into the dump bucket, bring a plastic cup into the tasting with you. When you want to spit, turn away from the group and use the cup. At the end of the tasting, empty it into the bucket. The third problem is that, like the professionals, you will have a better idea of what the wine is about than the people around you, who have the muffling influence of the alcohol. Your honest opinion about the wine can be unpopular. Maybe keep that to yourself. If you want to visit more than two wineries each day and you're not spitting, you have two choices, have a designated driver who DOES NOT DRINK anything, but water, an energy drink or maybe coffee. They cannot cheat. There have been numerous accidents when the 'designated' driver slipped up and sipped too much. Or you can hire a driver. Your transportation will cost less than the tastings, and it will keep you safer while improving your experience.

Sonoma American Viticulture Areas

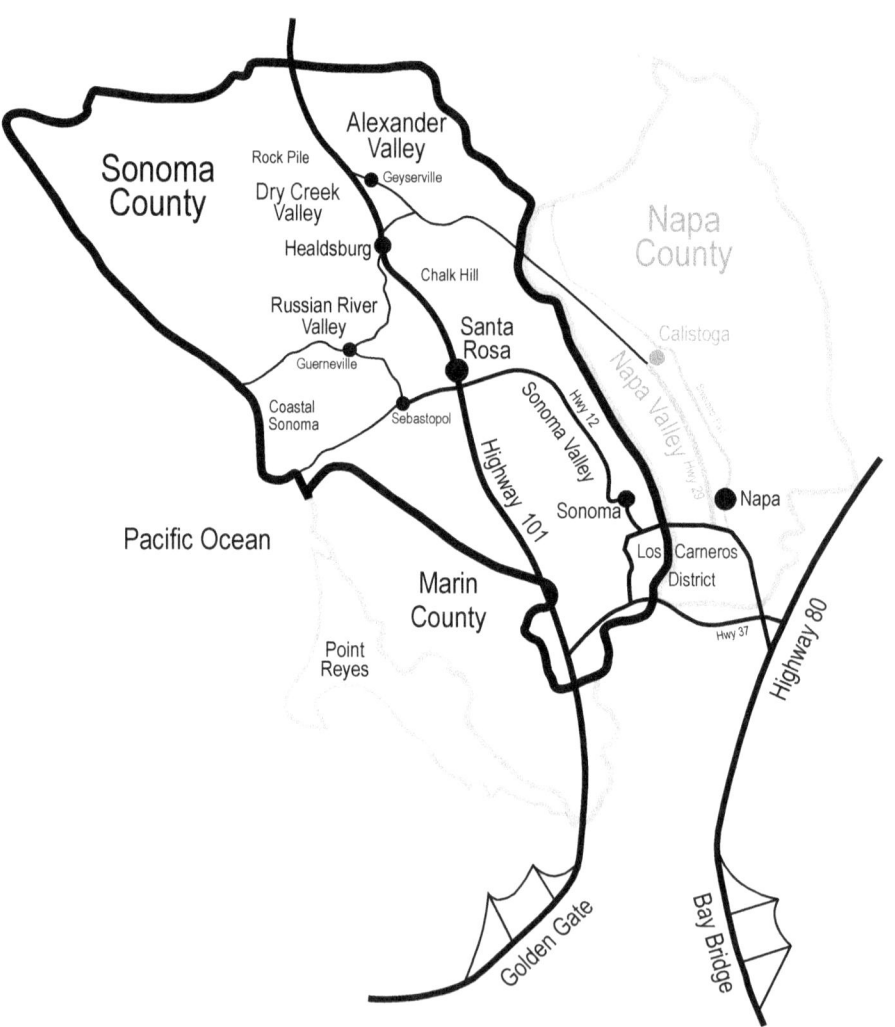

Chapter Four: Choosing Wineries Wisely

Many people who work in the tasting rooms love the subject of wine and are happy to share their knowledge, so be curious, friendly and ask questions! It's more fun for them when you have a good time!

If you want to learn more about wine, which is one of the biggest reasons people come to Wine Country, the tasting room is the best place. When wineries advertise for tasting room staff, the title they list most often is Wine Educator. Having someone who talks about the wine, where it came from, the conditions in the year the grapes were grown, the winemaker's style, etc., while you experience the wine is a tremendous way to learn. Not every person who pours for you will be able to answer every question. Everyone has a 'first day on the job' and this knowledge gap is more common at big winery tasting bars where they have high staff turnover. They have experts to train and mentor the team, but the least amount of education takes place at the big winery tasting bars.

Their big commitment to education is on their tours, seated tastings, and experiences. A small number of wineries do wine blending sessions where you leave with your own bottle. The person leading those understands the nature of each of the grapes you will be using, and the ways in which they interrelate. As you taste your way through that experience, you may feel like a first grader being handed a pencil the first time, but you will come away with a deeper knowledge of wine, scent and flavor that you will never forget.

Some of the best educators work at the smaller, exclusive wineries, after working their way up through the bar tasting scene. They work directly for the winery owners and they manage the hospitality side of the business, mostly pouring wine for collectors and coordinating the wine club. Most of the local wine experts are not sommeliers, a profession that developed because restaurants needed someone to manage the wine cellar. The people pouring wine come from diverse parts of the business with some of the best coming over from production. The wine notes that describe flavors found in a wine are the work of a Somm, because that is how they determine which foods the wine pairs well with as they help a restaurant patron choose a bottle.

An important part of the tasting experience are the buildings, their placement related to their vineyards, and the views they offer. A great deal of thought goes into creating remarkable experiences for the guests. Honestly, sometimes the experience is better than the wine. And sometimes the best wines are poured in the simplest surroundings.

Over the years tasting rooms evolved from kitchen tables, to bars made from boards spanning a couple of empty wine barrels in the winery's tank room, to walled off rooms that were less drafty and easier to light, to custom built hospitality buildings. There are still tastings at kitchen tables, although barrel and board bars are rare. But, as hospitality income became an increasingly important part of a winery's revenue, the tasting rooms became increasingly sleek. One of the most attractive qualities of the North Bay wineries is their incredible diversity and outright eccentricity. It seems like every possible type of hospitality space exists. Which is amazing, because the practical work of wineries requires certain design choices and the tasting rooms are often part of that same building. A winery needs to get the grapes in, move the liquid around and then get the wine out, all while keeping it clean and cool. But beyond meeting those basic needs, the buildings can express whatever theme the owner desires and can afford, and there are some highly creative and wealthy people in Wine Country.

There are styles that repeat and among the most interesting are the stone wineries from the 1800's that utilize gravity winemaking techniques, a handy feature when pumps were powered by strong hands and arms. Some of the most famous wineries, including Inglenook, Far Niente, Buena Vista, Beaulieu Vineyards, Beringer, Chateau Montelena and Charles Krug are in buildings from this period, although using modern equiptment.

There are a small number of California Mission Style buildings including St. Francis, Robert Mondavi and Groth, as was Franciscan prior to its transformation into the 'stark black and chains' Prisoner brand. There is a popular architectural theme of modern, minimalist natural wood buildings that are popular among the small ultra-exclusive wineries, a bit of understatement that harkens back to their country roots. These are practical buildings serving a specific purpose, so the combination of climate and the demands of winemaking make some materials better than others.

The most regimented design spaces in the winery process are the aging caves because they are moving heavy, fragile, and very valuable wood wine barrels in restricted spaces. But, even there, when the owners have sufficiently deep pockets and a vision, some amazing statements are made. For example, the elegant Katherine Hall Winery features great Belgian block and an impressive sculpture collection. Other notable 'statement wineries' are the Palmaz complex and the gardens of Landmark.

The choice of where to pour the wines varies. The smallest number are those that pour in their caves like Deerfield Ranch in Sonoma and Del Dotto in Napa. Others use spaces that look like fancy restaurants, like Ram's Gate in Sonoma and B Cellars in Oakville. Some go for the boardroom look, like Napa's iconic Shafer Winery and Cardinale, which encourages visitors to treat the wine as a serious subject as evidenced by their 'serious prices'. Some wineries belong in Architectural Digest, like Artesa, Domaine Carneros and the restored Buena Vista. Some are built around their views like Cade on Howell Mountain and Sbragia Family in Dry Creek. Some focus on their art collections like Imagery in Sonoma Valley, Peju and the Hall Winery in Rutherford. Some others we would kindly describe as rustic, hopefully without any snakes or scorpions, although we would caution you to watch your step.

When you choose the wineries to visit, the experience is just as important as the wines, otherwise you could have just had them ship the bottles to your house and saved yourself the trip. But when you visit these remarkable places you realize it was worth the effort. In many ways Napa and Sonoma are the quintessential American experience, a wide collection of native born and immigrant wine crafters who have pursued their dreams and opportunities and now want to share them with the world, for a little profit.

Chapter Five: Our Best Tasting Room Tips

What will the tasting room host expect from you? They'll expect you to enjoy! They do not expect you to be a wine expert, that's their job. As a wine tourist, what are you an expert about? The wines you like! That's because you have a library of scents and flavors from every wine you have ever tasted. The limbic part of your brain, where scent, flavor and emotion live, never forgets those experiences, including where you were and how you felt. Your wine preferences are uniquely yours, based on that amazing mix of deep memories, adjusted for your evolving physiology. That's because the sensitivity of your senses changes over time as your nutritional demands shift.

One of the first questions we ask new clients is their age because of the evolution of the palate. We suggest places that make wines that are appealing to their generation, but with some exceptions. For example, while younger people generally like light bodied wines like Chardonnay, Pinot Grigio and Pinot Noir, those working in high finance often go for the expensive Cabernets. Those are normally an older man's wine; full flavored, tannin rich and suited to a less sensitive palate that craves sulfur. Another example: we normally expect the Boomers to like those Cabs, but if they are fitness enthusiasts, their healthier, hyper-sensitive palates often prefer white and sparkling wines.

There are good reasons why the most often heard phrase in tasting rooms is, "The best wines are the ones you like".

They typically pour four to five wines, starting with a high acid white to clean the palate, followed by increasingly bigger and darker wines, saving the most expensive for the end. Each sample is supposedly one ounce. If they are using the same glass for the entire tasting don't worry about the flavors mixing, since each stronger flavor overwrites the previous. Don't rinse the glass with water between wines because the water coating will interfere with your tongue's sensitivity.

Sometimes the lineup of wines are arranged side by side in multiple glasses. This gives them time to open up properly and it lets you revisit them. Vertical tastings of the same wine from different vintages were once more popular. This is a European tradition for wineries that make one wine, where different years produce varied results. But North Bay wineries, thanks to the remarkable climate, have a wide variety of high-quality wines to show off, and visitors who are adventurous in their tastes.

Bigger wineries have wider selections of wines, both standard and reserve lists, plus food pairings. Smaller wineries have one list. Don't assume the reserve wines will taste better. They are chosen because they age well, and their current flavors may be less appealing.

Not all tasting room staff are equally knowledgeable. In the slow season, the managers and professionals are pouring, but in the Summer, less experienced, part-timers often work in the tasting rooms. Ask your concierge or tour guide to recommend a particular host who is known for their knowledge and fun style.

The amount of time they spend with you depends on how busy they are. Year round on the weekends, large wineries can be slammed but even in the high season, especially during the week, there are plenty of small wineries looking for guests. If you want to learn more about wine, do the seated tasting, because hosts often only work with one group at a time, so you get more personalized attention.

The typical lineup starts with a white wine such as the popular Chardonnay, especially in cooler Sonoma. It is a muscular grape that handles higher alcohol levels, that can be made crisp in stainless steel tanks, or barrel aged for a toasted, buttery caramel flavored wine, with hints of chocolate and nuts. Those buttery Chardonnays were a gateway wine for many beer and spirit drinkers because that collection of flavors is remarkably similar to Coca Cola.

In Napa, a popular first wine may be Sauvignon Blanc which grows beside the Cabernet and Merlot. Locals like it because it ripens earlier, so it doesn't compete for production tank space and it's ready to sell the following Spring, while the other wines are still aging in their barrels. Fermented in stainless steel, it makes a crisp, refreshing low alcohol wine that goes great with lighter fare.

When it is aged in new, toasted oak barrels it produces the smoky Fume' style. While most people drink it young, laying a good one down for a decade produces wonderful depth and smoothness with a honeyed nose. Harvested late, after it has been desiccated by the botrytis fungus, it becomes the costly, golden sweet Sauternes.

Other possibilities for a first wine, depending on location and the winemaker's need for a diversion, are Pinot Grigio, Riesling, Chenin Blanc, or a signature blend. Tasting Hint: It is important to manage your alcohol intake. If you are not a fan of white wines, ask your host to skip them. Next come the red wines, from lightest to heaviest. In cooler areas like southern Napa, and southern and coastal Sonoma, that's Pinot Noir and Syrah.

In the warmer sections of Sonoma, Petite Syrah and Zinfandel are popular. In the warmest areas (Napa Valley and Alexander Valley) the grapes of Bordeaux rule: Cabernet Sauvignon,

Merlot, Cabernet Franc, Malbec and Petite Verdot. Here and there you will find a few pockets of Italy's Sangiovese and Barbera, and Spain's Tempranillo. But please realize that we are dramatically understating the possibilities of what you might taste, because over a hundred different grape varietals thrive in the diverse and hospitable North Bay climate.

There are numerous heritage vineyards planted by the orginal immigrant generations containing obscure varietals. Just over the eastern hills from Napa, Portuguese families planted their own varietals that thrive in the windy Suisun Valley. This wide variety, coupled with excellent quality, makes the North Bay Wine Country a popular destination for the grape varietal adventurer, and yes, that's a thing!

Chapter Six: Ralph's ABC's for Tasting Wine

The way you drink wine with a meal is different from how you sample it in a tasting room. The funny techniques you see people using during tastings help them perceive the wine better through the senses of sight, scent and taste. It starts with the glassware. Wineries use crystal goblets because they are rougher than glass. When you swirl the wine, those microscopic bumps pull apart its molecules, mixing them with oxygen, releasing the aromas and flavors for you to experience. Hint: The fancier the winery the fancier the glasses.

Start by holding the glass by the stem. It is partly to prevent your hand from warming the wine, but mostly because that makes it easier to move the wine around inside the glass. Temperature matters and wines are poured at different temperatures; sparkling and sweet whites are the coldest while the dry whites and light reds are cool. The big red wines start out at 'cellar' temperatures and then gradually warm during the tasting, which allows the complex flavors to bloom. The worst thing you can do is not give the wine a chance to open up and stretch, after its long seclusion in the bottle. That's like having the genie pop out of the lamp and not giving them time to properly introduce

themselves before you start asking them to grant your wishes.
Start by holding the glass upright and taking a sniff. Much of what you're smelling at the top of the glass is alcohol rising off the liquid. Next, set the glass on the tabletop (the tasting notes make a nice, soft surface), place your fingers firmly on top of the base and vigorously swirl the wine clockwise. Now, pick the glass up and hold it to the light. Wine is a complex creation so you may see red, blue, violet, gold, straw and so on, depending on the varietal. Set the glass down and swirl it again.

Next, pick up the glass and hold it at a 45-degree angle across your body (so you avoid pouring the wine on yourself), and put your nose on the glass' lower lip, and take a sniff. At this angle, the alcohol fumes are rising inside the globe, and slipping out at the top like smoke going up a chimney, happily bypassing your nose. Now, instead of mostly smelling alcohol, you're smelling the heavier fruit flavors below, the wonderful scent of fermented grapes!

Take a moment to appreciate the bouquet. With a big, densely flavored red wine, it's best to repeat the swirl and sniff steps a few times, until you've truly captured the fullness of the scent, before taking a sip. With a white wine the flavors open more quickly and you can move through swirl, sniff and sip in three lovely steps. Then just keep repeating the process until there is none left.

Wine Geek Alert! There is an odd phenomenon that happens with wines that have been aged in oak for an extended period, usually eighteen months or more. As related to me by winemakers, when you swirl the wine clockwise you will smell predominantly fruit flavors. But when you swirl counterclockwise, you will also notice the nutty, sometimes spicy flavors that come from the barrel. Why does this happen? According to Ralph's best quasi-scientific analysis, it is due to the relative efficiency of vortices. A clockwise swirl more efficiently mixes the various part of the wine together. But the less efficient counterclockwise swirl allows the layers to separate. The wooden barrel flavors are the last ones to be infused into the juice and in this less organized mix, some of those woody notes are left floating at the top for your nose to discover. This technique is used by some winemakers to determine a barrel's influence on the wine. If you have a good sense of smell, you will notice the difference. Now you are officially a Wine Geek!

When you take a sip, move the wine around your mouth, so it touches all your taste buds from the tip of your tongue to the valley in its center, and then, both sides. Once the flavors are well dispersed, you can swallow the sip. There are certain scent notes that are only released when they touch your tongue. To access them, gently breathe in through your mouth so the aromas on your palate reach your nose via the back of your throat. There is another quality you should note called 'mouth feel'. It is how the texture of the wine feels to the surface of your mouth. Is it sharply acidic, soothingly silky, or almost sticky and syrupy?

That gives you some clues about the kinds of foods and situations the wine is suited for. A high acid wine goes great with food because it cleans the palate and helps the digestion. A wine with a soft mouth feel is nice at a party for socializing. The syrupy sweet wines make a nice dessert after a heavy meal, when you don't have room for cake.

One 'mouth feel' to watch out for is the almost flame-like touch of a high alcohol, dry wine, which is why that kind of wine is called 'hot'. Port is also high in alcohol, but the wine is heavy and sweet, so the alcohol is deeply embedded in the flavors. But, many of the most expensive Cabernet blends are quite hot, at 15% to 16% alcohol, while totally dry (meaning that all the grape sugar has been converted to alcohol). If the dehydrating alcohol is not well moderated and integrated into the wine, it will feel like a sip dries out your tongue and you may be thirstier after the tasting than before you began.

With these steps, you have experienced almost the full signature of the wine; the look, scent, flavor and feel. The only note still missing is how the alcohol hits you. Popular wines range from about 10% up to 16% alcohol. Port is fortified with grape spirits to stop the fermentation before the sugar is completely consumed, and it is about 20% alcohol. A wine below 12% is called a table wine, and for many years most wines were in that range. The change happened due to the desire for bigger, fuller flavored wines, which requires leaving the grapes on the vines longer, where they make more sugar, which the yeast converts into more alcohol.

Related to inebriation, not every wine makes you feel the same. We suppose this is because wines are chemically complex nutrition and your body uses the dietary components it encounters. The best wines are also the healthiest, because they are pure, they contain a higher quality alcohol and more vital nutrients, so your body recognizes it as 'good' food. Eating more vital foods helps you feel optimistic, confident, content and loved. This is not scientifically quantifiable, but it is clear from experience that some wines make you feel 'better' than others.

The Importance of Swirling

We cannot repeat this enough, swirling is essential. A great deal of effort and technology goes into keeping the wine away from any oxygen that will dissipate its flavors. Mixing the wine with air inside the glass releases those trapped aromas and flavors, making them available to your nose and tongue. Swirling the glass by sitting its base on a tabletop produces much better aeration than swirling it while you hold up in your hand. It also keeps the wine stains off your clothes, which happen most often later in the day when you loosen up. Even the best wineries don't have carpets in their tasting rooms for a reason.

The nose detects millions of scents, many more than we can identify. But the palate is more limited. Conventional wisdom says there are only six or seven main flavors that people can describe. You have probably heard the list; sweet, sour, salty, bitter, pungent and astringent with 'umami' being a recent addition. We detect more nuances, but flavors defy verbal description because they are experienced in the body's language center and they take up the full band width. That's why great flavors can render you speechless. It's hard to describe a taste in detail because 'flavor' is its own language.

The First Sip Conundrum

While all these techniques sound thoroughly enjoyable, there is a hurdle to overcome. That first sip of the day rarely tastes good. Why? Because much of what you will be initally tasting is your breakfast, or maybe your toothpaste, still stuck on your tongue! The same thing happens after lunch, but to a lesser extent. The wineries know about this, so that is why they start with a high acid, white wine, to clean your palate and warm up your taste buds. Once your palate is clean and tuned it's clear sailing.

It is important to give your nose and palate time to wake up and adapt to the situation so do not rush the first tasting. In your everyday life those two sensory organs experience the same group of scents and flavors in the same sequence with little variation. They are nice aromas, familiar flavors, comforting to your emotions and sometimes delivering valuable messages, like that afternoon cup of coffee when you need to get back to work. At a wine tasting you are asking your palate to analyze a series of complex wines containing hundreds of scents and flavors, one after another. So start off slowly and don't worry, it's like playing a sport, after a little warm up, you will find that everything moves. feels and even tastes right.

Sonoma & Napa Main Roads

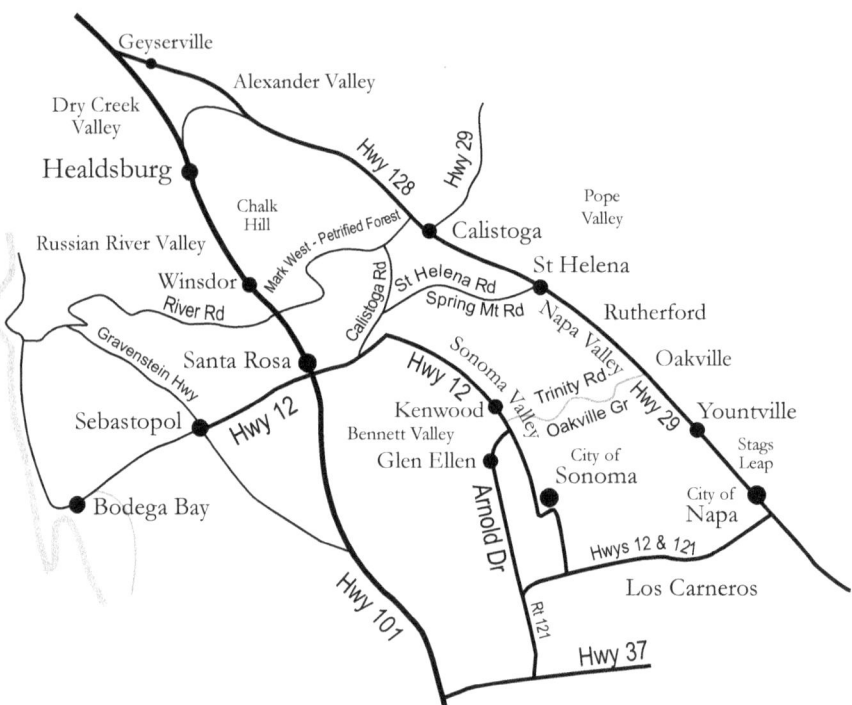

Chapter Seven: Navigating Sonoma

From the Golden Gate Bridge, southern Sonoma County is a thirty-minute drive north through Marin County. As compared to urban San Francisco and suburban Marin, Sonoma is made up of small towns, farms, ranches and vineyards, fit between oaks, laurels, pines and expansive redwood forests.

Sonoma produces vegetables for their many restaurants, apples in the Russian River Valley, small grows of cannabis, hops for their renowned craft beers, dairy for their artisan cheeses, Petaluma's prized poultry, and beef cattle grazing the bucolic, green hills of coastal Sonoma, plus honey from their many flowers.

But premium wine grapes are their biggest crop, grown in eighteen American Viticulture Areas (AVAs), spread across a county more than twice as big as Napa. Not surprisingly, winemaking is their biggest industry with over five hundred wineries. The most visited wine regions are Los Carneros, Sonoma Valley, Russian River Valley, Dry Creek Valley and Alexander Valley.

The differences between the various growing regions are remarkable, thanks to Sonoma's two coastlines: one along the cold, deep Pacific Ocean, and another along the shallow San

Pablo Bay. Their influence makes every valley, line of hills and mountain slope climatically unique. These sit atop a checkerboard of diverse geological structures, caused by the meeting of volcanic uprisings and ancient basalt seabeds cut by numerous rivers and streams. The result is the world's most varied premium wine region, that grows over a hundred grape varietals.

In comparison, Burgundy France produces primarily four or five varietals, Champagne produces three, Bordeaux about ten and Napa about fifteen. Sonoma's coastal Pinot Noir and Chardonnay compete well with Burgundy. The Cabernet Sauvignon and Merlot of Alexander Valley hold their own against Napa and Bordeaux. Even less widely planted grapes like Sangiovese, Grenache and Zinfandel, produce wines that compare well to the places where those grapes have grown for centuries. Sonoma was able to accomplish this since the 1820's, when the first vines were planted, due to its remarkable location.

This same combination of terrains, crossed by hills and waterways, makes navigating the region challenging. But when you know what to expect, it becomes easier. Let's start with the name Sonoma, which signifies the 'Valley of the Moon', and it applies to the crescent-shaped, fifteen-mile long Sonoma Valley, that is bisected by Highway 12, Sonoma Highway, and bordered by Arnold Drive to the west, which you can often take to avoid traffic congestion.

What's in a Name?

Sonoma is also the name of the little city that sits at the base of the valley, so often, when people say they are going to Sonoma, that's where they mean. It is also the name of the county, which is bordered by Marin to the south, Mendocino to the north, Napa to the east, and the cold, Pacific Ocean to the west, which sends fog banks sweeping over the land nightly. So, when you say you are going to 'Sonoma', it helps to be specific!

For wine touring, we divide the county into North and South. The historic town of Sonoma is the center of the southern half and elegant Healdsburg is the center of the northern half. The city of Santa Rosa, which spreads over a wide plain, is the economic midpoint. When deciding on a day trip, for the sake of time and distance, plan to visit wineries in either one region or the other.

The Important Roads You Need to Know

Highway 101 is a major highway that crosses the Golden Gate Bridge from San Francisco and intersects **Highway 37** abeam of southern Sonoma. **Hwy 101** also intersects **Highway 12** in Santa Rosa and further north, River Road, which travels west through the Russian River Valley. **Hwy 101** also intersects **Healdsburg Avenue** and **Dry Creek Road** which connects to the northern most wine valleys, Dry Creek and Alexander.

Highway 37 starts at **Highway 101** and travels east, ending in Solano County at **Highway 80**. It intersects **Highway 121** North at Sears Point (Landmark: Sonoma Raceway and the 'turbo cow'). **Highway 121** is home to numerous popular Los Carneros wineries, and it intersects **Highway 12 North**, which goes north to downtown Sonoma and the Valley. *Taking **Highway 101N** to **37E** to **121N** to **12N** is the quickest and prettiest way from the Golden Gate Bridge to downtown Sonoma.*

Highway 121 is combined with **Highway 12** for a short distance, before continuing east into Napa County and intersecting **Highway 29**, Napa's main road.

Highway 12 travels North through downtown Sonoma. It continues north into the heart of the 'Valley of the Moon', including the towns of Glen Ellen and Kenwood. It goes through the outskirts of the city of Santa Rosa where it intersects **Highway 101**. Then it continues west into downtown Sebastopol, intersecting **Highway 116**.

Highway 116 also intersects **Highway 121** in Los Carneros and merges with **Highway 101** in Petaluma. It then splits off in Cotati and goes northwest through Sebastopol. Then it travels through the Russian River Valley as **Gravenstein Highway**.

It passes through Guerneville and becomes River Road, heading west until it ends at **Highway 1, the Pacific Coast Highway**.

River Road intersects **Highway 101** north of Santa Rosa. It travels on the river's southern bank, through the heart of the Russian River Valley, ending at the **Pacific Coast Highway**.

Healdsburg Avenue intersects **Highway 101**. The 'Downtown' exit brings you to Westside Road, which travels south into the northern part of the Russian River Valley. Going north on **Healdsburg Avenue** brings you through the downtown. Then it intersects **Dry Creek Road** which goes north into the Dry Creek Valley. **Healdsburg Avenue** also continues north through the west side of the Alexander valley. North of town it intersects **Alexander Valley Road**, which goes into the eastern side of the valley and continues south into northern Napa.

A Helpful Note About Very Convenient Los Carneros
See Map C on Page 194

The thin slice of land at the top of the San Pablo Bay, that spans Sonoma and Napa is called Los Carneros. Its wind-whipped, basaltic, highly drained vineyards are planted like a carpet with Pinot Noir and Chardonnay, in a continuous swath of precise green lines.

The area got its name from an early 1800's Spanish land grant, because the cool winds blowing off the bay make these rolling hills a good place to raise 'los carneros', or sheep. It is unique among the North Bay American Viticulture Areas (AVA) because it is shared by two counties, Napa and Sonoma, but the consistent climate, geology and exposure make the designation appropriate on both sides of the county line.

Los Carneros has often been called the American Burgundy because it produces so much of America's premium Pinot Noir and Chardonnay, although the strong winds produce a higher acid wine that goes best with food. Truthfully, Sonoma's Russian River and Pacific Coast wines may represent a truer comparison to Burgundy's earthy style.

But Los Carneros is home to some wonderful wineries and well worth the visit for their bright and refreshing wines. The fact that it is so convenient to San Francisco makes it a popular daytrip destination. Many of the first 'Carneros' wineries you encounter in Sonoma coming north see hordes of visitors, so they price their wines accordingly. But when you go a little ways off the beaten path you will find numerous premium producers.

Navigating Sonoma is easy because there are not many roads, but the actual driving can be tricky because wine country roads tend to be narrow, winding and sometimes bordered by thick forests. So, take your time, enjoy the scenery and be safe!

The Sonoma Valley Overview

Chapter Eight: The Sonoma Valley
See Map D on Page 195

The Valley of the Moon is a crescent shaped slice of heaven that extends northwest from the Carneros Highway. It includes the three adjacent towns of Sonoma, Aqua Caliente and Boyes Hot Springs, as well as Glen Ellen and Kenwood further north. South of the Sonoma Plaza the valley has a broad, flat floor and due to the bay's influence, the climate favors the cool-loving grapes like Pinot Noir and Chardonnay. North of the Plaza the valley narrows, and the protected hillsides promote a wider selection of varietals, including the warm-loving Sauvignon Blanc, Cabernet Sauvignon, Cabernet Franc, Merlot, Zinfandel, Sangiovese and numerous Rhone varietals. The Valley ends at the plains on the southern side of the City of Santa Rosa, the county seat.

The valley's central road is Highway 12, Sonoma Highway, which goes north from Carneros Highway through the towns, and then continues through the northern valley, where it is the main wine road. Close to the picturesque Sonoma Plaza there are three other wine roads. To the west is Arnold Drive which starts in Los Carneros at Highway 37. Along that stretch of road Arnold is home to Southern Sonoma's busiest wineries, Ram's Gate, Viansa, Jacuzzi, Cline, Gloria Ferrer, Anaba, Schug, Roche and Robledo.

Arnold Drive then travels north, parallel to Highway 12, until the two intersect in the town of Glen Ellen. Farther north, Arnold passes the tasting rooms of the little town of Glen Ellen and the nearby, biodynamic Benziger Winery. Arnold Drive bypasses the three southern downtowns making it a favorite alternate route on busy traffic days. To the south of Sonoma Plaza is 8th Street, the local industrial district where industry means winemaking and numerous small wineries make their homes there. These include the 'Eighth Street Wineries' located in small warehouses at the Sonoma Skypark. Some have tasting rooms and others are only open to the public during seasonal events. The third wine route is Napa Road, which travels from east to west south of the Plaza. It quite appropriately is the road from Sonoma to Napa, not to be confused with Napa Street, one of Sonoma's main streets at the south edge of the Plaza. At the southeast end of Napa Road, you will find Scribe Winery and Nicholson Ranch.

Sonoma Plaza
See Map A on Page 192

The valley and the town of Sonoma are economically linked to the world by the Sonoma Highway (Hwy 12), because unlike Napa, there is no river to promote commerce. The Plaza, and its surrounding streets, are California's most historic location because it is the home of California's twenty-first and final Franciscan Mission, the Spanish military barracks, and the site of the Bear Flag Rebellion monument. To the east of the Plaza, next to the Sebastiani Winery, is the 'Town Vineyard', where the missionaries first planted vines in the 1820's. Further east is California's first modern winery, Buena Vista, established in the mid-1800's, and nearby is their contemporary, Gundlach Bundschu. Sprinkled around California's largest Plaza is a wonderful collection of restaurants, shops, galleries and of course, tasting rooms. On the Plaza are picnic grounds and a Visitor Center in an old Carnegie Library. The layout of the paseos (passageways) and courtyards with their stucco and ceramic tiles gives the town the feeling of what it once was, a Mexican Pueblo at the northern tip of the Spanish empire.

It is from the Coastal Miwok and Pomo tribal languages that Sonoma translates to "Valley of the Moon". Coincidentally the narrow northern valley is shaped like the crescent moon and its rich soil makes it better at retaining moisture than the surrounding valleys and nearby Los Carneros. Those intimate dimensions make it a charming drive and there are numerous friendly, well-established wineries that reside there. In the first edition of this book we recommended the Sonoma Valley for the first-time visitor, and a Napa innkeeper objected, saying it would divert traffic from them. But we still feel that way, because the wineries are spread out, with forests and country homes in between, so visitors never feel overwhelmed by a profusion of well-known labels, one after the other. The experience is relaxed, Bohemian and traditional, the wines are good and reasonably priced.

The Sonoma Valley has been farmed by the same families for generations, so it has that comfy confidence that comes from knowing who they are and where they belong. Its popularity is helped by being an incredibly convenient destination from much of the Bay Area. The town of Sonoma sits in the southern third of the Valley, with wineries in all directions, but the largest concentration starts five miles north of the Sonoma Plaza on Highway 12, beginning at the Madrone Road traffic light. There are four wineries near this intersection, Abbot's Passage (site of the historic Valley of the Moon Winery), B.R. Cohn Winery, Little Family, and Hamel Family. Around the next curve is Imagery, which produces small lots of unusual wines and has a unique, curated wine label art program. They share a driveway with low key Arrowood Vineyards.

Further north just off Highway 12, on Dunbar Road are three small, unique wineries. First is Loxton Cellars, where you walk past the press and tanks to get to the bar, and where you can taste with the winemaker. Next door is Wellington Cellars and down the street is Lasseter Family, owned by the head of Pixar. Further north are the caves at Deerfield Ranch, and across the road you will see the expansive vineyards of the Kunde Family. Next up are the widely distributed Kenwood and Chateau Saint Jean (pronounced 'Jeen') Wineries, both of which sit beyond their vineyards. Across from St Jean is Saint Anne's Crossing, a popular stop for the Zinfandel lovers. For the visitor, one of the most important is VJB Vineyard, because it makes an idyllic spot to taste their wines outdoors in an Italian-style Piazza with a delicious lunch from their deli, outdoor barbecue or pizza ovens! Wellington Cellars is their 'sister winery'. As you head farther north, at the next corner is Landmark Vineyards with their beautiful gardens, started by members of the John Deere family but since sold to new owners. Down that road is the diminutive La Rochelle Winery tasting room with their lovely garden. Coincidentally, both wineries specialize in excellent Pinot Noir and Chardonnay. At the top of the valley at a rare traffic light is the Saint Francis Winery, with its charming California mission-style building and stunning views of Sugar Loaf Mountain and Mount Hood. Just past there is the Ledson Winery, a dramatic looking building and popular wedding venue.

For lunch or dinner there are numerous restaurants in downtown Sonoma, Glen Ellen and Kenwood, as well as store front tasting rooms and markets. Tucked up in the hills are more wineries that are open by appointment. If you plan to picnic, we suggest buying your supplies early and keeping it in a cooler, because the lunchtime lines can be long and slow. You can't bring food to any venue that serves their own. If you want to have an early dinner, which is always a good idea on a wine touring day, downtown Sonoma is a great place for that. Here, farm to table is the norm, not the exception. The 'Wine Country Casual' dress code applies in the restaurants, so generally the style that you wore to go wine tasting works fine for dinner at all but the fanciest restaurants. More importantly, bring something warmer to wear in the evening because once the sun begins to set, it cools down quickly even on the hottest day.

Chapter Nine: Northern Sonoma & Healdsburg
See Map H on Page 199

Not many years ago, Healdsburg was a quiet farming town that served an important support role for the many farmers in the three nearby growing regions, Russian River, Dry Creek and Alexander Valleys. That changed in the 1970's when northern California winemakers shifted away from making cheap jug wines in favor of premium varietals, which attracted tourists. Because nearby Santa Rosa is the primary commercial hub, the smaller, countrified Healdsburg was ripe for a tourism upgrade.

The transformation was less extreme than Napa Valley's Yountville, where private homes and rundown bars, gave way to new hotels and restaurants. Healdsburg held onto more of their history and personality, and the result is a charming plaza surrounded by a mix of old and new. Besides attracting a steady stream of tourists, the changes also attracted new prosperous residents. If Healdsburg were as close to San Francisco as downtown Sonoma, it would be as busy, but the two-hour drive on Highway 101 to the downtown exit filters out the less serious enthusiasts. Healdsburg led the way in encouraging storefront tasting rooms. Many local towns discouraged them, deciding that those activities should stay in the valleys. They didn't want the competition for the bars and restaurants, and they didn't want drunken tourists staggering down their streets. But Healdsburg dealt with a special circumstance. The nearby wineries are predominantly small, family affairs situated on narrow, winding, heavily forested roads, with neighbors who like their quiet surroundings. The expense of converting farm buildings into legal tasting rooms can be prohibitive, and their neighbor's objections can stall their projects for years.

Downtown tasting rooms have proven an economical alternative and they have become an important part of the scene! The amazing diversity of varietals grown locally allows tasting rooms to establish unique niches. The result is a remarkably wide selection of varietals available to taste, all within strolling distance of each other. Healdsburg has good hotels, bed and breakfasts, inns, and a wonderful restaurant scene, plus plenty of upscale shopping. Like most of the Wine Country towns, as compared to many tourist areas, it has a large full-time population, because the wineries are big employers. While there are houses that tourists can rent, most Wine Country towns strictly regulate that, so the selection is small.

Getting There from the Bay Area

Highway 101 is the main North Bay highway and it goes right through Healdsburg. Do your best to avoid rush hours which, fortunately, are predictable and short lived. During the Summer, late afternoon southbound traffic on Highway 101 through Santa Rosa is often heavy. Consider having an early dinner locally, then driving south when the traffic and your inebriation level is reduced.

Driving from Downtown Sonoma and Napa Valley

Just past Sonoma Valley's northern end, its main road, Highway 12, intersects Highway 101 in Santa Rosa providing a scenic route between the two towns. Coincidentally, at the northern tip of the Napa Valley, Highway 128 goes northwest through

Sonoma County's Knights Valley into Alexander Valley. There, it becomes Alexander Valley Road which diverges from Highway 128 and connects to Healdsburg Avenue just north of the downtown.

The Three Valleys Around Healdsburg

The area around Healdsburg is filled with numerous small, family wineries, growing diverse varietals in three distinctly different valleys. Russian River Valley is the coolest of the three, so most of the Chardonnay and Pinot Noir vineyards are found there. But it is a big region and there are warm pockets where Zinfandel, Rhone and Bordeaux-style grapes are grown.

The Dry Creek Valley is a small slice of warmth, insulated from the Pacific Ocean fogs and the cool influence of the Russian River. They are famous for Zinfandel, but they also grow other warm-loving grapes. Alexander Valley is wide and long, bordered by hills, making it the warmest of the three valleys. It is also home to the largest wineries and renowned for Merlot, Cabernet Sauvignon, and other Bordeaux varietals. But it is a big growing area, so numerous other popular varietals thrive here. Like much of Sonoma, this area was planted by Italian immigrants that produced wine grapes for home winemakers during Prohibition. They planted red grape varietals that would harvest early, ship well and blend together successfully, including Petite Sirah, Grenache, Alicante Bouschet, and Zinfandel. They also planted numerous obscure varietals that are found in legacy vineyards and sometimes defy identification.

Getting to the Valleys

The Russian River Valley is south of Healdsburg, Alexander Valley is off to the east and Dry Creek is west of town. The northern edges of the Russian River Valley transition into the other two which makes it the most amorphous. For example, while its cool, western reaches are dominated by Pinot Noir and

Chardonnay, the warm northeastern tip grows Cabernet and Merlot, much like the Alexander Valley, which is to the northeast of the Russian River. Russian River's southern Olivet Lane section is home to old vine Zinfandel, much like Dry Creek which is due north. The lines between the three are often blurred.

Getting to each valley from downtown Healdsburg is easy. One of the main Russian River Valley's wine routes is Westside Road, with connects to Healdsburg Avenue at a circle on the south side of town. Dry Creek Road, that valley's main route, intersects Healdsburg Avenue on the north side of town. Taking it north will bring you to the top of the valley. Parallel to it, across the creek, is West Dry Creek Road, which has fewer wineries and more twists and turns.

Healdsburg Avenue travels north from the downtown along the western side of the Alexander Valley. Just north of town is the expansive Montage Resort. Just north of there the avenue intersects Alexander Valley Road on the right, which will take you into the eastern parts of that big, broad sunlit space. Farther north, Healdsburg Avenue ends and Geyserville Avenue continues north, parallel Highway 101, connecting many of those larger wineries together. Neither Dry Creek nor Alexander Valley have many roads so they are easy to navigate.

If you are being driven by a professional guide who knows the roads you can visit wineries in all three valleys in a single day. But, if you are driving yourself, visit one valley, maybe two, if your winery picks are close by because navigating the area is tricky and both the wines and the experience are intoxicating. The Healdsburg area is remarkably lovely, with a tremendous diversity of environments and grapes. There is less traffic, so the tasting rooms and restaurants are less stressed. Our recommendation is to visit Healdsburg from Southern Sonoma or Napa or, better yet, stay in one of the local hotels to enjoy the area in a way that feels like home.

Chapter Ten: The Russian River Valley
See Map E Page 196

This region is named for the river that flows south through the Alexander Valley, the Dry Creek Valley and then turns west in the Russian River Valley, on the way to the Pacific Ocean. Imperial Russia established a settlement on the coast in the 1800's to grow food for their settlements in Alaska. Eventually, their 'Fort Ross', or 'Rossiya', named for Mother Russia, became the base for a profitable fur trade. Their settlement attracted other Eastern Europeans, including the Korbel brothers, whose winery continues making popular sparkling wines in Guerneville. Sparkling wines are generally made from Chardonnay and Pinot Noir grapes and those varietals thrive in the bright sunshine and cool climate that the Pacific Coast happily provides.

The North Bay's unique climate is shaped by the great depth of the ocean just offshore, which delivers cold water to the surface. When the hot sun heats the ocean's surface, massive fog banks form, which flow up the river channel overnight, cooling the grapes and drenching the redwood forests. While many sections of the Russian River Valley are planted with vines, the vineyards atop the hills closest to the sea, safely above the fog line, grow some of America's most famous and expensive Pinot Noirs, but there are few tasting rooms there.

The two sides of the river feature different geological compositions because the soft riverbed sits at the line where a harder volcanic intrusion from the north, met a soft, basaltic seabed in the south. Those northern rocky hills are crossed by narrow, winding roads that snake around steep slopes, heavily forested with evergreens and redwoods. The vineyards often occupy steep hillsides, producing small, deeply flavored berries. On the river's south bank, the gentle rolling hills are more easily planted. The trees are mostly deciduous, and the water table is high, which allows the growers ease and flexibility in their grape varietal choices.

The wineries are found in clusters spread around the valley. Just south of Healdsburg, along the Highway 101/Healdsburg Avenue corridor, are a small but significant group of about twelve wineries including Foppiano, Rodney Strong, J Vineyards and numerous smaller wineries. Much further south, in the town of Fulton where you will find the tasting room for Kendall-Jackson. To the east of Healdsburg is a remote, but interesting part of the Russian River Valley because the warm, northeastern tip of the valley is climatically similar to the Alexander Valley, which is immediately to the north. But unlike Alexander Valley's wide, flat floor, Russian River's Chalk Hill is on the rocky western slopes of the Mayacamas Mountains. It was only in the 1970's when the adventurous Chalk Hill Winery began planting these less hospitable slopes that it became popular.

They were attracted by the chalky soil, like that found in numerous French white wine regions. But the Mayacamas is geologically varied, so they eventually found other slopes where they could also grow the popular premium red varietals. Now, there are several other premium producers there, including Roth Estate, Lancaster Vineyards and Verité Winery. Note: Chalk Hill Road is a slow ride with many twists and turns, so plan accordingly. The rest of the Russian River wineries are found in four general groups southwest of Healdsburg. Those on the northern (west) bank of the river are reached via Westside Road. The northern part of Westside Road, just south of Healdsburg, is the border of Dry Creek Valley and the Russian River Valley, Watch for the signs. In that stretch of road, south of the downtown on Westside Road, are a string of small wineries including DaVero Farms, Mill Creek Vineyards, Armida (the southern-most Dry Creek Valley winery), De La Montanya, Twomey (owned by Silver Oak) and Matrix (owned by the Wilson Winery), Then you come to Flowers (owned by Quintessa), Bacigalupi Vineyards, MacRostie Winery, Landmark at Hop Kiln Estate, J. Rochioli Vineyards, Gracianna, Arista, Williams Selyem, Thomas George, Porter Creek, Moshin and Gary Farrell.

Between Porter Creek and Moshin Vineyards, Westside Road intersects Wohler Road. *This helpful road crosses the Russian River over a narrow, but scenic bridge, and intersects River Road,* giving you access to the wineries on the south side of the river. Before you get to River Road, Wohler Road intersects Eastside Road, which travels along the east side of the river, giving you access to several excellent wineries including Kistler Vineyards and Copain Wines. The Russain River turns from south to west near Wohler Road. The River Road wineries include Woodenhead, Joseph Swan, Martin Ray and Martinelli Vineyards. River Road also intersects Slusser Road, which brings you to two big wineries, La Crema at Saralee's Vineyard and Sonoma-Cutrer.

Olivet Road

The next cluster of about ten wineries sits on the rolling hills around the short and very straight Olivet Road, which runs from River Road in the north to Guerneville Road in the south. This area is known for its high-water table and gently rolling hills. These are all small wineries, mostly family owned. While the featured grapes are Pinot Noir and Chardonnay, there are numerous old Zinfandel vines here and there. The collection of wineries there include Harvest Moon, DeLoach, Benovia, Inman, Pellegrini, and Battaglini.

Gravenstein Highway

The next cluster of wineries are southwest of Olivet Road, along and near to Highway 116, known locally as Gravenstein Highway. That interesting name comes from an apple varietal that was once prevalent in the local orchards, and there are still plenty of apple orchards growing here, so pick up a pie. Highway 116 runs northwest from Sebastopol to Guerneville, where it intersects River Road. But most of these wineries are within a couple of miles of each other, between Occidental Road in the south and downtown Forestville in the north. They include Merry Edwards, Iron Horse, Paul Hobbs, Furthermore Lynmar, Emeritus, Fog Crest, Dutton Estate, Dutton Goldfield, Taft, Balleto, Hanna and Kobler.

The Outliers

West of Forestville there are few accessible wineries, other than Hartford Family and Korbel on River Road just east of Guerneville. Korbel was founded in 1882 by three Czechoslovakian brothers. At the time it was an eight-day trip in ox carts to bring their wines to the docks in Petaluma. Today the ride to their redwood encircled estate is much faster. They have a deli and tables. It is important to plan your lunch in advance, there are restaurants in the towns of Healdsburg, Sebastopol, Forestville, Graton and Guerneville. There are also picnic tables but check if the winery you are visiting has a place to picnic and if you can bring food, or if you can buy it at the winery.

The Russian River Valley is a delight to visit and it is so large and varied that you can easily spend an entire day touring there. The wineries are small, friendly, mostly family owned, and their wines are wonderful. But, navigating those small, twisting roads can tricky, so careful planning goes a long way towards creating a dream tour. Note: A short distance north of downtown Guerneville is the popular and beautiful redwood forest, Armstrong Redwoods Reserve. Also, check out our bonus story about the name 'Russian River Valley' at the back of the book.

Chapter Eleven: The Dry Creek Valley
See Map F on Page 197

The Dry Creek Valley is a small, almond shaped slice of heaven aligned from northwest to southeast, with Lake Sonoma at the top, the 'Dry' Creek in the center and the Russian River at the bottom. The valley sits to the west of downtown Healdsburg, but most of the wineries are located to the northwest.

It has two north-south roads on either side of the creek. Dry Creek Road starts north of downtown at Healdsburg Avenue. It also intersects Highway 101. It is a relatively straight road and most of the wineries are along its length. The road changes names near the Lake Sonoma Dam, where it turns west and heads towards the Pacific and becomes the amazingly winding Skaggs Creek Road.

Parallel to Dry Creek Road, on the other side of the creek, is West Dry Creek Road. That starts at the southern edge of downtown Healdsburg, on the other (west) side of Highway 101, coming off Westside Road. It travels north the length of the valley, ending just below Lake Sonoma. Its path is narrow and twisted so avoid it unless you are going to a specific winery.

Westside Road

The half dozen wineries at the valley's southern end are mostly on Westside Road, so they are easily accessed from the south side of Healdsburg. A fun one is Armida Winery, situated inside a pair of geodesic domes atop a steep hill, overlooking the valley. Another pretty location is Orsi, just outside town in a building that has been home to several wineries.

If you are visiting the wineries on Westside Road and want to see more in the northern part of Dry Creek Valley, bypass winding, narrow West Dry Creek Road and take Highway 101 North to the Dry Creek Road exit. In the upper valley, there are just two crossroads connecting those parallel roads, Lambert Bridge Road at the valley's center and Yoakim Bridge Road to the north.

The terroir of Dry Creek is perfect for grapes, a warm, narrow valley with low hills on either side. Grapes like a steady daytime heat and Dry Creek Valley has the advantage of being insulated from both the cold, foggy Pacific Ocean, and the Russian River that brings cold water south from the Mendocino mountains. The valley's compass alignment and narrow width makes it perfect for capturing the morning sunlight that produces bright fruit flavors, while the western hills shade the grapes from the bleaching effects of the afternoon sun.

Over the hills to the east is Alexander Valley. To the west, the forested, rocky hills continue uninterrupted to the Pacific Ocean twenty miles away. Many of the early farmers in the area were Italians who came to work at the Italian Swiss Colony Winery in the 1800's. Fortunately for them, during Prohibition, the home winemaker market exploded, and Sonoma growers tripled their production shipping them grapes. Zinfandel was one of the most popular Prohibition varietals because it harvested early and shipped easily. There are few places where Zinfandel grows as well as Dry Creek, and as a result, of the three local valleys, Dry Creek is the most densely planted.

The valley has numerous similarities to popular Sonoma Valley to the south. It is about the same size, proportion, and compass orientation, and of the three nearby valleys, it is the most convenient to the downtown. Both valleys grow a nice collection of warm weather grapes that yield the kind of solid income that promotes winery longevity. Both are formed around streams, rather than rivers, so they do not suffer the seasonal flooding that the Alexander, Russian River and Napa Valleys do. Both Healdsburg and downtown Napa have suffered floods due to nearby rivers, but the Dry Creek and Sonoma Valleys have avoided that debilitating problem. But there are also differences between the two little valleys.

Dry Creek Valley is a bit warmer, so even in winter, it feels milder than the surrounding areas. Sonoma Valley is filled with larger, well established wineries, spread out through its length. In comparison, Dry Creek is mostly filled with small, family owned estates that sit close to each other. In many cases, the families have owned the land for generations, selling their grapes to the local wineries, before the kids or grandkids built a winery.

Dry Creek Valley is remarkably pretty, and its history produces an experience that is relaxed and hospitable, making it a long time favorite of the professional guides. Navigating the valley is easy because the southern wineries are on Westside Road and the northern wineries are found on, or near, three other roads; Dry Creek, West Dry Creek and Lambert Bridge. *Landmark: The Dry Creek Store is at the intersection of Dry Creek Road and Lambert Bridge.* There are two very enjoyable wineries on Lambert Bridge Road; Dry Creek Vineyards and the Passalacqua Winery. Ironically, the charming Lambert Bridge Winery is not on that road, but on West Dry Creek Road just south of there. Just north of the intersection of Lambert Bridge Road and West Dry Creek is the A. Rafanelli Winery and the biodynamic Quivira Vineyards, with their educational garden.

Zinfandel vines in Dry Creek are easy to spot because they are usually grown as individual bushes, rather than being trellised. Even though Zinfandel may be the valley's hometown favorite, they also produce high quality Cabernet Sauvignon and Merlot. Many wineries also feature good Chardonnay and Pinot Noir, because they are so close to the nearby Russian River vineyards.

There is one large wineries in the valley, Ferrari-Carano. It sits near the top of the valley on Dry Creek Road. The multi-story hospitality building is a dramatic, Italian-style villa with wonderful views, surrounded by gardens. However, the winery was built in a Japanese style. The Carano family owned a casino and some of that style shows up here. Since you are in the neighborhood, visit Sbragia Family Vineyards, located just north of them. They have the best views of the valley from their patio.

There is another big winery in the valley, a massive operation owned by the Gallo family for their premium Sonoma brands. It does not host visitors, but it is cool to know about. As you drive north on Dry Creek Road approaching Lambert Bridge Road, you can catch a glimpse of it on the right.

Just south of there, at the intersection of Lytton Springs Road, is the Mauritson Winery which specializes in Zinfandels from their hillside vineyards in Rockpile, near the Lake Sonoma Dam. Lytton Springs Road is the way to Alexander Valley, and on the way through the low hills, you will see the fun Mazzocco Winery and the renowned Ridge Winery at Lytton Springs, known for their stellar Cabernet blends.

Many of the wineries have picnic tables, so bring your lunch with you. If you are visiting during the week, you can grab lunch and sit at the Dry Creek Market, but in season, or on the weekends, it can be a long wait to get your sandwiches. In downtown Healdsburg there are several places to pick up supplies, with the Oakville Market, on the corner of the Plaza being the most well-known. Because Healdsburg has a large year-round community they also have large super markets if you need more, as well as plenty of nice restaurants around the plaza.

Most of the wineries sit beside their vineyards, but there is a 'collective' winery area in a former fruit-drying yard called 'Timber Crest Farms'. It includes some fun wineries that you can walk between, including the delightful Amphora Winery and the Papapietro-Perry Winery, well-known for their Pinot Noirs.

Dry Creek Valley and Alexander Valley are parallel, although the Alexander Valley is wider and longer. They are connected by three roads over the low hills, but the two significant ones are Lytton Springs Road and Canyon Road, where you will find the generations-old Pedroncelli Winery. You can combine the Dry Creek and Alexander Valleys in a single day tour. The Francis Ford Coppola Winery, with their great restaurant, is in Alexander Valley north of Canyon Road, so it is easy to pop over there for lunch (reservations are suggested) and a tasting, and then head back to Dry Creek.

It is also nice to combine Dry Creek with the tasting rooms of downtown Healdsburg, which adds some downtown meal possibilities. With that said, Dry Creek has more than enough to entertain you for an entire day. Being too ambitious about how many wineries you visit in a day often short changes winery experiences that deserve more time.

Northern Sonoma Overview

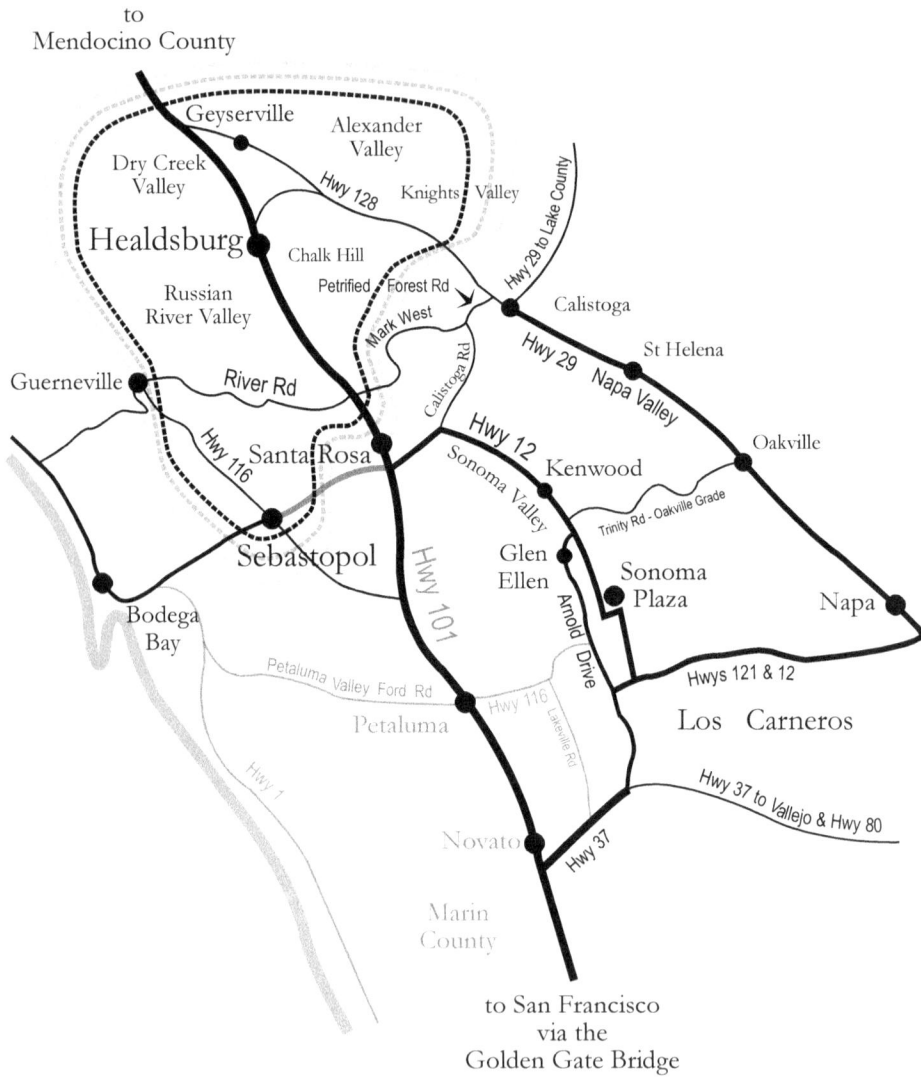

Chapter Twelve: The Alexander Valley
See Map G

Before westerners came to the Alexander Valley the tribes there were called the Pomo and the Onosai, or the 'Outspoken Ones'. The Spanish called them the Wappo, from the Spanish word Guapo, for handsome and brave. They had pushed their villages south into the Napa Valley, gaining control of obsidian deposits there, a volcanic glass from which wickedly sharp knives, arrowheads, and axes were made that they could both use and trade.

The first westerners who came to the valley were mercury miners during the gold rush, looking for 'Quicksilver', that was used for refining the ore. They traveled north from the mines on Mount Saint Helena, on a trail over the low hills into lovely Knights Valley, and then through a series of narrow passes into the southern Alexander Valley.

They found themselves at the western face of the volcanic Mayacamas Mountains, the same range that forms Napa Valley's western border. Around Geyserville, the region's volcanic nature is evident, with tremors being a common occurrence. The winery, Geyser Peak, took its name from steam spewing from a nearby mountain that has, for the moment, calmed down.

After the miners left, the farmers came. They looked at the sunny, broad valley floor, watered by the meandering Russian River and promptly planted wheat and raised cattle. That kind of farming and ranching requires large swaths of land and even today, most of the properties on the valley floor are expansive. The valley wraps around Healdsburg from where it meets Knights Valley in the east, stretching up to the town of Cloverdale in the northwest. Pretty little Geyserville sits in the middle of the valley and it has some nice inns, restaurants and tasting rooms.

The Russian River is not obvious as you travel the valley, but it has shaped the valley's floor by changing its course over the eons and depositing pockets of well-drained gravel under the rich soil. This is ideal for growing Cabernet Sauvignon, which likes having dry feet. In comparison, when Merlot is grown by the river, the vines use the heavy, water absorbent clay to form big, juicy berries. While there are other varietals growing nearby, these two are the big moneymakers.

When folks began planting grapes here in the 1970's, Kendall Jackson and Gallo quickly jumped in and were soon followed by other large wineries but there are numerous small family wineries here as well. For example, in the eastern hills above the lovely Robert Young Winery are the charming Garden Creek Ranch Vineyards and the up and coming Skipstone Ranch. North of Jimtown are the Foley Sonoma Winery and deLorimier. Across from Coppola is the very traditional Trentadue Winery.

Navigating the Valley

Alexander Valley is the easiest of the three valleys to navigate because Highway 101 travels its length, with convenient exits at the important spots and it is paralleled by straight local roads. The quickest way between these spread-out wineries is often on '101'. The southeastern part of Alexander Valley Road (Highway 128) is home to a line of wineries; scenic Hanna Vineyards, Alexander Valley Vineyards, Silver Oak's environmentally efficient, state of the art facility, and the Stonestreet Winery, that sits, like a monolith on a bare rise. Stonestreet is the (Kendall) Jackson family's premium estate, where they use grapes from the northeastern hillsides across the road. When Highway 128 heads north to Geyserville, Alexander Valley Road continues west to Healdsburg Avenue, passing the entrance to the prestigious Jordan Vineyards. Farther north, on the west side of the valley alongside Highway 101, are three large wineries; Francis Ford Coppola (their restaurant, Rustic, is the only place to eat in the valley), Clos Du Bois Winery (closed) and Trione. Landmark: The large white structure on the eastern hillside is the River Rock Casino parking garage.

Two important factors shape the valley's flavors. They are the northeast to southwest orientation of the valley that aligns it with the setting sun, and the low western hills, that allow the strong afternoon sunshine to bake the valley floor vines. That bleaching sunlight forces the Merlot to produce more tannins, making the wines more structured. Meanwhile, the Cabernet is grown on the valley floor on forgiving gravel rather than rocky hillsides, so it produces somewhat softer wines. A muscular Merlot and an approachable Cabernet is the opposite of what most Cab lovers expect, but they are a tasty find. The classic style Cabernets, earthy, deep and needing time to age, more often come from the rocky hillsides, where the vines struggle to produce small, richly flavored grapes.

Thanks to the diversity of these three valleys, the Healdsburg area has become an important California wine center. The rising popularity of Pinot Noir accelerated their success. Only its greater distance from San Francisco protects it from being overwhelmed by visitors. While the casual tourist staying in San Francisco tends to visit the more convenient wineries to the south, the enthusiasts make the effort to drive a little farther to this gem of an area. Many repeat visitors live in the Bay Area and they appreciate the region's wide selection of wines and experiences that are casual, enriching, and affordable.

*If you come to Wine Country with your honey
and it doesn't make you feel romantic,
you're not doing it right!*

Answer A: You Gotta Eat!

The Italians are among the world's oldest winemakers and they firmly hold to the belief that wine is food, not a thing apart. And winemakers everywhere know that the locations that make good wine grow other delicious items too. Thus, it is only natural that another good reason to come to Wine Country, besides the wine is for the food. There are wonderful markets and restaurants for you to enjoy in both Napa and Sonoma, but Napa is unique because it has more Michelin-starred restaurants per capita than any place else on Earth. That's quite an accomplishment for a small, agricultural county. Researching where to eat is a complicated process unto itself, and a bit of a moving target because restaurants come and go. Here we are concerned primarily with what you are going to eat during a day of visiting wineries.

We are not leaving you completely on your own about choosing when and where to eat. In the maps, we note the best markets to pick up lunch supplies. Because markets serve the locals year-round, not just the visitors, they don't change too much. Historical note: The Oakville Grocery in Napa Valley opened in 1881 and it is the oldest continuously operating market in California.

As for the restaurants, we note the towns where you will find them. The choice of whether to eat at a market or a restaurant depends on the day. If you have a professional driver, because you want to visit as many wineries as possible, order your food in advance and eat at a market because it takes less time. If you are driving yourself, the sixty to ninety minutes spent in a lovely restaurant, drinking sparkling water (no wine) with food, is a healthy, happy way to manage your alcohol consumption. Whenever possible, make a reservation.

When you are touring wineries and consuming alcohol, the success of your day depends on what and when you eat. This chapter covers the essentials. You may be thinking, 'If there is something I know about, it's eating". True! But wine touring is a sport that you only play occasionally and it comes with its own stresses and strains. To play it successfully you need to consume the correct nutrients, on a schedule, to keep your body happy and sound. Here is how you manage that!

Water

Hydration is very important because alcohol is dehydrating. Bring two to three bottles of cold water for each person in the car to drink between wineries. One of Ralph's most repeated phrases is, "The secret to a good wine tour is how much water you drink!" Normally consume one ounce of water for each ounce of wine. On hot days it is common for the humidity levels to be twenty to thirty percent, so people lose significant moisture through their skin. On those days you may need to drink up to two ounces of water for each ounce of wine consumed.

Breakfast

Before a tour, always have a good breakfast that includes protein and fat. Adding a little toast is okay but avoid high carb meals like pancakes with syrup and fruit. It is helpful to understand that alcohol is post-digested sugar so adding sweets to that can make you 'loopy' pretty quickly. You need to allow plenty of time to arrive at the first winery by 10 am and driving often takes more time than GPS says, so always add at least 15 minutes for the winding roads and the wrong turns caused by the nearly invisible signs. If you are visiting Napa and Sonoma from the east coast, due to the time change, you will be up at the crack of dawn so make time for an early breakfast, then go back to your room and get ready for the day.

Lunch

Plan your lunch before you go out the door and choose a location within fifteen minutes of the wineries. If you're picnicking at a winery (many don't permit that, so check), get your lunch supplies on the way to your first stop to avoid the lunchtime rush at the markets. If you're going to a restaurant, make a reservation. By the way, those breadsticks at the wineries are not meant as food. Their purpose is to scrub the young tannins off your tongue, so the wines don't all taste the same. If you are doing a food pairing, don't expect that to replace a meal. Due to local regulations, those portions will be small.

Dinner

Wine tasting is hard work. It combines socializing, travel, walking and intense sensory experiences far beyond what you normally experience. You will be tired. Our suggestion is to plan your meal before the tour, place your order early and pick it up on the way back and have it on your patio. We've lost count of the number of guests who blew off dinner reservations at fine restaurants after a wine tour because they fell asleep. If you really want to eat out, plan an early casual dinner immediately after the last winery, near your hotel.

The Importance of Protein and Fat

Why do we keep suggesting a high protein, high fat meal, maybe with some crusty bread? Because alcohol is a great solvent for the two densest energy sources, protein and fat. That's why wine with a meal, especially meat or fish, helps your digestion. On the day of the tour, if you follow our advice, about 30 minutes after lunch you'll get a second wind. Also, by giving the alcohol something to break down, you will neutralize some of its inebriating effects and greatly improve your tasting endurance. Warning! Most cheeses are not a good protein and fat source when wine tasting, because they may contain too much sugar. Alcohol is made from sugar digested by yeast, so both are absorbed into the system quickly. Tasting endurance is about maintaining gradual (aka slow) assimilation.

Wine Headaches

These happen more often with red wines because the higher tannins are especially dehydrating. But cheap sulfites, bad winemaking techniques and dirty grapes may also be the culprits. You can tell the difference between the causes of the headaches by the location of the pain. Pain in the center of the head is dehydration. The first solution is to drink more water to hydrate the brain. Next, find a cool spot out of the sun and chill for a while. To prevent that happening in the future drink more water and wear a hat.

When the pain is in the forehead, which may be accompanied by tightness at the back of the neck, that is most likely caused by a histamine reaction due to dirty grapes with too much MOG, material other than grapes, getting into the mix. That can be leaves, twigs, bugs or just dirt. It can also be due to bad winemaking, which usually means a poorly managed fermentation.

All red wines have natural sulfites that act as a preservative. But in cheaper wines they are added to destroy bad bacteria, and those sulfites can be a problem, causing headaches and flushing. Because white wines don't sit on the skins they are lower in tannins so you may want to drink those instead.

To relieve those symptoms, drink a stimulant like a strong cup of coffee or an energy drink. Alternatively, take an OTC antihistamine with lots of water. Cool down in the shade and it will improve. To avoid wine headaches in the future don't drink cheap wine.

Answer B: Clothing, Wine Country Casual

When you are tasting wine, you will be more relaxed if you do not wear white, yellow or any color that shows a wine stain like a red wound. Patterns are a wonderful alternative.

One of the questions that often comes up from clients is "what to wear?" Or should we say, what NOT to wear. Please leave the high heels and dress shoes at the hotel. Vineyards are farms and ranches and while many of the more famous wineries have 'theme park-like', city-shoe friendly paving, many others are better suited to running shoes, flats, or sandals. Also, some of the most famous wineries are big, spread out properties that require plenty of walking, as well as stairs for you to navigate, probably while feeling tipsy. When picking a shoe for the day, choose comfort and safety over style.

Please save the lipstick, perfume and cologne for dinnertime. Tasting rooms celebrate the senses of scent and taste and anything that competes with the wine's flavors needs to be avoided, not only for your sake, but for the enjoyment of the other guests. Also, lipstick carries its own taboo, because the compounds affect the wine's flavors and getting lipstick marks off of fragile crystal tasting glasses presents a problem for the wineries. Foregoing the lip gloss and perfume will be appreciated by the tasting room staff who are pouring for you and therefore it will affect the way that they treat you. Having a friendly host adds immeasurably to your enjoyment and may even result in an extra pour of some hidden delight, so a little consideration of them is politic.

Wear loose fitting, comfortable clothes. You're going to be sitting in cars, walking and maybe hiking a bit for a tour. For most of the year, except in winter, Napa and Sonoma are about fifteen degrees warmer than San Francisco, and the farther you go up the valleys away from the bay, the warmer it gets. People can be sitting comfortably outside on the winery patios in Los Carneros, while thirty miles North in Calistoga, Sterling is shutting down their gondola on their hilltop winery, because it's too hot to use their outdoor tasting bars.

In the Summer, if we begin the tour in Los Carneros, we'll suggest that the clients bring a light jacket or sweater. But by lunch time, the jackets have been tossed in the back and I'm handing clients cold bottles of water. While some wineries are air conditioned, many prefer the open air feeling and when possible, they host their guests outside at tables. A few wineries host their tastings in their wine caves, which can be cool, but not cold because they typically have spaces designed for hospitality, not just wine storage. No winemaker wants people coming and going in their inner sanctum all day, messing with the temperature and letting in bugs. While a wine cave is usually about 60 degrees, a hospitality cave is a bit warmer, so it is comfortably cool.

Good sunglasses are a must, because the weather channel lists six levels of sunlight for the North Bay, calling the highest 'Abundant Sunshine'. Extreme solar radiation is one of the keys to why this region makes great wines. Most of the grape's flavors are made from sunlight and wine grapes, due to their thick skins, need the sunlight to be as bright as possible. The difference in comfort levels when standing in the sun versus the shade can be dramatic, which explains why there are so many shade trees near the wineries. We've often selected our summertime wineries based on the availability of shade. It can be a long, hot and bright wait for clients in our SUV without a friendly tree. Also, if we have our client's purchases in the car, we'll need to keep the air conditioner on the entire time to prevent damage to the wine. Normally, if we are not in the winery, we like to sit in the car, with the engine off and the windows open, with a laptop. When else do you think we have time to write these books? Be prepared for sunset, because as soon as the sun goes behind the mountains, the temperature drops and all those layers of clothes you took off earlier go back on.

> *Wine Country Casual at its best means classy, but comfortable. There's never a problem with looking too good, but you can look too formal.*

Travel Hint: Choose clothes that are comfortable both in the car and the winery. Summertime temperatures during the day normally top out in the late afternoons in the 80's or 90's, with very low humidity, and then drop into the high 50's or low 60's overnight as the fog rolls in off the bay. When choosing your clothing, it's helpful to remember that this is a very elegant and prosperous farm country. Behind the scenes, it is a land of pickup trucks and big SUVs. Jeans, flannel shirts, cowboy hats, baseball caps and practical shoes reign but, in the tasting rooms and restaurants, it is casually elegant. You can rock a Hawaiian shirt, slacks, or a skirt with a pair of sockless loafers or sandals.

In hot weather, shorts and polo shirts for men are perfectly fine. Women of course have more latitude, but comfortable, casual and classy works really well. Hint: No matter how often we suggest practical clothes, sometimes girls just like to dress up. So, if you are planning a day in high heels and short skirts, choose wineries on the valley floor where the paths are smooth and the walk to the tasting room is short, and don't schedule a long walking tour!

Another hint: If you show up in old, ragged shorts, a T-shirt and flip flops, they'll still pour wine for you, but they may not take you as seriously.

Winter

Wine Country greets visitors year-round, even during the rainy season from December through March. After all, it doesn't rain inside the tasting rooms, and summer's parched hills turn emerald green in winter. Many locals feel that it's more beautiful in the winter, when it looks like Ireland, with the mist clinging to the hills. In the summer it looks like Tuscany, golden and glorious.

If you're visiting in the winter bring a light jacket and an umbrela. If you forget one the hotels and wineries keep umbrellas on hand in case of rain. Depending on where you are staying the amount of rainfall varies widely. Napa Valley gets about twenty to twenty-five inches of rain annually. Sonoma, being closer to the ocean gets more, and the Sonoma coast gets about fifty inches, which is why there aren't many wineries there as wine grapes mostly like it dry.

While it might be wet, it won't be too cold during the day, normally in the 50's and 60's. The coldest days are in February. In between the rain we still have our abundant sunshine, and during those beautiful, sparkling days of winter, the personal attention you'll receive at the quieter wineries and restaurants makes up for the lost opportunity to wear shorts.

Answer C: Find the Grapes You Love

Grapevines have long genetic codes that let them quickly adapt to new environments and conditions. The code is so complex that if plants had become the animals, the grapes would have been the humans. Grapevines are an important part of our culture. In the Old Testament, Cain and Abel's first jobs were herding animals and tending vines. What kind of vines do you think they were tending? The Norsemen named America's northeastern coast Vinland, for the grapes they found there. Two thirds of the world's grapes are used for wine and they are grown in every American state, including Alaska where they're moved inside for the winter.

Many of the world's European-style vines are grafted onto American root stock to protect them from Phylloxera, a root boring mite to which the native American vines are resistant. The mites spread from North America to Europe in the 1800's, devastating millions of vines, until a grafting solution was developed. As an aside, Thomas Jefferson failed in his efforts to grow European Vitis Vinifera grapes in Virginia. But then, two hundred years later, two Italian winemakers, using a grafting technique from northern Europe, succeeded. Now there are more than three hundred wineries in the Virginia hills.

Why are there thousands of grape varietals? Because that highly adaptable genetic code encourages them to mutate in reaction to changing conditions. In a vineyard, one vine may unexpectedly produce something different, like grapes of a different size, better drought or disease resistance, bigger productivity, or higher quality. Or it might be a totally useless trait! If it's a 'good different', growers propagate cuttings from that mutation called 'clones', and future vineyards might be planted with that vine. For example, the Italian Brunello grape is a clone of Sangiovese, with smaller, more flavorful berries. The mutation financially transformed that region for the better. Here is another example. Zinfandel suffers from inconsistent berry maturity, where too many bitter, immature grapes go into the wine. The two ways to make better Zin were to sort grape by grape, which is expensive, or ripen bunches more, which produces excessive alcohol levels. UC Davis developed a clone where the bunches ripen evenly, a dramatic improvement.

Grapevines are not planted from seed but grown from cuttings. Why? Because modern vineyards have no 'boy and girl' plants, only hermaphrodites! Why? Because males don't produce grapes and females produce too many! Hermaphroditic vines naturally grow half as many grapes, which is preferred in winemaking! Also, since they have both types of sex organs on every plant, in the absence of bees, breezes will carry the pollen to nearby receptive flowers. If they grew vines from a seed, that would produce either a male, a female or a hermaphrodite. But cuttings produce an identical version of the original plant. Here is an interesting thought. Because growers have planted the same popular varietals for generations, the Pinot Noirs you drink today are later clones of the same Pinot that the ancient Romans enjoyed.

When vines are moved to a vineyard with a different geology and weather, they go native and become something unique. Sometimes they find friends. Cabernet Franc and Sauvignon Blanc vines cross pollinated spontaneously, producing Cabernet Sauvignon, a grape with thicker, more flavorful skins and larger production. Rioja Spain's red grape, Tempranillo, is genetically related to Cabernet Franc, and thus Cab Sauv, yet it tastes different. Were the vines first brought from Spain to France, or the other way around?

In Napa and Sonoma, we know where the grapevines came from. Among the first were the Mission grapes, a sweet, low acid berry that was planted by the Spanish in 1820 near the Sonoma Mission in 'Alta California'. Later General Vallejo, the commandant, sold two thousand vines to George Yount, a former mountain man and wagon train guide, who was the first to plant vines in Napa. A Hungarian Count, Agoston Haraszthy, brought hundreds of European varietals to his Buena Vista winery in the 1850's. Unfortunately, Phylloxera eventually devastated his vineyards.

Eventually the region was helped by the grafting, and as sea captains and adventurers settled in Napa, they planted varietals that they knew from their travels, the grapes of Burgundy, Bordeaux and Germany, although the cool-loving Riesling has mostly disappeared. The many Italians who settled in the North Bay chose early harvesting, marketable grapes. In warmer Napa, Zinfandel was their main grape, but in Sonoma's Piedmont-like climate, they also grew Grenache, Petite Syrah and Alicante Bouchet, medium-weight reds that shipped and blended well.

It was a long wait before some adventurous growers would introduce their own Italian varietals, Sangiovese and Barbera, and the number of plantings is still small. In Napa, Pinot Noir and Chardonnay, the varietals from Burgundy, were originally grown in the warm heart of the valley. But a thin-skinned grape like Pinot ripens so quickly in that heat that the vines don't have time to infuse the berries with their deep flavors. So, in the 1970's those varietals moved to the cooler area of Los Carneros, originally touted as America's Burgundy. But granting that title was premature because its basaltic soil lacks complexity, although its winds produce the acid levels that make a good 'food wine'. Los Carneros is the only AVA shared by the two counties and it's mostly planted to Pinot Noir and Chardonnay used in both still and sparkling wines, plus some Syrah, Pinot Grigio and other cool loving grapes. The wineries on the Sonoma side of Los Carneros lean towards large production, affordable wines and attractive, spacious hospitality centers. On the Napa side are primarily premium wineries, tucked away in the rolling hills. As Pinot's popularity increased, cool coastal Sonoma and Russian River Valley wineries proliferated. The combination of ocean influence, complex geology and great forests produce spectacular wines. Now, numerous small, charming producers of Pinot and Chardonnay, with their delicate flavor signatures, and the easier price tag, consistently attract the Bay Area's young, successful tech community.

In Napa, from the city of Napa to the valley's bottleneck by the town of Saint Helena, the Bordeaux varietals rule. Those include, Cabernet Sauvignon, Merlot, Cabernet Franc, Malbec, Petite Verdot, Sauvignon Blanc and Semillon. The lion's share goes to Cab Sauv, which accounts for more than half of Napa's vines. North of the bottleneck, the valley's warmest region grows Bordeaux varietals, along with a continuing tradition of Zinfandel, recognizable by its bush-like shape. Growers there are increasingly planting more heat-loving varietals.

Sonoma County has a tradition of innovation and eccentricity. It is three times bigger than Napa County, and more climatically diverse which allows them to grow over a hundred grape varietals. The hilly Sonoma Valley grows the widest collection of varietals including Bordeaux, Burgundy, Rhone and Italian styles. This narrow fifteen-mile-long valley, north of the Sonoma Plaza, is one of the world's most popular wine regions, elegant and yet casual, and it is always fun. From the Russian River Valley west is Pinot and Chardonnay land. Northeast Alexander Valley favors Merlot and Cabernet and the little, charming Dry Creek Valley produces some of California's best Zinfandel. Wine Country is big and spread out, so go to where they grow the grapes you love!

Answer D: Transportation

Sometimes the best solution when you are drinking is to hire someone to drive for you. There are numerous options. Let's start with the most legitimate, regulated, and respected, professional drivers and guides that are licensed by the Public Utilities Commission, and commercially insured.

They will have their TCP number on their cars, websites, and business cards. They are the standard of the personnel transportation industry. There are two types. The most visible are the companies that follow the traditional limousine model of black cars, drivers in suits, with fleets that run from cars to buses.

When you call their 800 number, they will find you a safe vehicle and a drug tested driver. In Wine Country they have three downsides. First, they are generic. Second, each company has a small core of drivers who are experienced wine country guides, and a much larger group of drivers who are new, less experienced and part time. The problem is, when you book a car you don't know which type of driver you are going to be spending the day with. The third issue is that they are the most expensive type of personnel transportation.

A more exclusive version of this is the professional, TCP licensed guide who drives their own commercially licensed vehicles, most often a luxury SUV that deals with the country roads well. They are highly skilled and knowledgeable and usually less expensive than the big companies, even though they provide a superior experience. That is because they don't have large advertising costs, working almost entirely by referral.

They will help you plan the tours, make recommendations and appointments, answer questions about the region and the industry, and share a local's perspective. They don't wear black suits, but instead show up in the kind of comfortable, casual clothes that lets them blend in at the wineries, where they know many of the people who work there. The downsides are that there is a limit to the size group they can handle and they may only do wine tours, so they won't pick you up at the airport and it takes research to find them. These are family businesses so they may have only one or two guides, so if they are booked on your date, you'll need to call someone else. But, since they all know each other, they'll likely recommend another guide.

Obviously, since we've worked in the tour business for many years, and this is our model, we are biased. But honestly, the private guides are the Rolls Royce of the hospitality industry. They are the region's smallest group of tourism professionals and they typically have large, loyal clienteles. Wine Country is a big, complicated place and finding what you want takes research, which for these guides is an ongoing process. Also, navigating a rural area where so many people are drinking and driving is challenging, so having a professional driver is a big advantage.

A fun alternative to driving up from San Francisco is the boat from the iconic Ferry Building to Vallejo, a city at the northeast corner of the bay at the mouth of the Napa River. It is a scenic hour trip on the water and most transportation companies are happy to meet you there.

Group Tours

There are San Francisco and Wine Country based bus tours that do generic itineraries of commonplace wineries. We don't recommend them because they don't give you an honest view of the place. They too easily turn into booze cruises where the winery hosts talk at you, not to you. The wine culture is deep, and education is paramount, so people come to Napa and Sonoma from all over the world to work and learn. You don't see that side of the place stepping off a wine-soaked bus, surrounded by a crowd of strangers. That doesn't mean buses don't have their place here. This area is a favorite for corporate and family events, where a day in Wine Country is a chance to get folks together, for networking and celebration. Those events are all about hospitality, something which this area does very well. Having group tastings and a catered meal in a wine cave with your friends and colleagues is something to remember.

We Drive Your Car Services

The "We drive your car" services cost about 20% less than the private guides. They are required to have a TCP license, which demands periodic drug testing and very expensive commercial insurance that wraps around the client's rental car. That's because the commercial insurers do not like the safety records that come with smaller cars. Approach them with due diligence, because we have seen times where they let their license and insurance lapse but kept working with clients. Make sure you can verify that they are operating legally, otherwise steer clear.

Hiring a Cab

There is a new wrinkle thanks to the Ride Share economy. When you book a Cab, they require a credit card, and there is a hefty cancellation fee. That is because people so often call a taxi for a ride, while using their ride share app. Half the time when the cab arrives, the customer has already left in the ride share. Cabs are not cheap, but if you arrange for them to pick you up, they will be there on time. Because they have no minimum time requirements, like the tour companies, you can use them as an adjunct on a tour. For example, at the end of the day you can have your tour driver bring you to a restaurant and then take a cab back to your lodging. That way you are not paying an hourly rate for a guide to sit in their vehicle while you eat. Usually, the price of the cab can be a savings if the restaurant is not far from your hotel, but check their rates to be sure.

Ride sharing exists in Wine Country on the weekends, primarily at the big, valley floor wineries on the main roads between the city of Napa and St. Helena. On busy days it can be a long wait. They resist going to the small hillside wineries because these part-time, non-professional drivers often get lost. GPS is not very dependable in these mountainous areas. We've seen too many Ride Share drivers smoking cannabis while they wait, which may be another reason they get lost. If you go to a mountain winery in a ride share, you may be stranded there, due to poor phone reception, or difficulty finding a driver willing to take the long ride up into the hills. Ride Share is not practical for the adventurous visitor, or for high-end tours with precise appointments.

Answer E: The Art & Science of Winemaking

People have been making wine for generations, passing the knowledge from parent to child, but up until the 1800's the mechanism that makes alcohol was considered akin to magic. In the United States, Louis Pasteur is esteemed for his development of Pasteurization to inhibit food spoilage. But in France he is beloved for discovering which 'tiny sparks of life' contribute to a great bottle of wine and which ones screw it up.

Pasteur's research into microbes led to wineries becoming obsessed with cleanliness and to doctors washing their hands. During his work developing Germ Theory, he had an ongoing debate with Antoine Béchamp who developed Terrain Theory. Pasteur postulated that health was attained by killing the 'bad' microbes. Béchamp proposed that microbes were opportunistic and one could maintain good health by promoting the supportive microbes with diet, exercise and lifestyle, which naturally inhibits the destructive versions.

This debate continues between the pharmaceutical and natural health industries, but in wineries it is settled. Growers generally accept the importance of 'terroir' or terrain, because research has determined that a vineyard's distinctive flavor owes much to the health of the soil's microflora. That is determined by how it is farmed, the nutrition it receives and the animals and plants and that live there. Also, no one questions the importance of microbes, and premium winery sanitation equals most medical facilities, at least any place where the wine is touching. So, for winemakers, both Pasteur and Béchamp were correct.

Because of Pasteur's work, ninety percent of winemaking is washing equipment, nine percent is record keeping and one percent is wine tasting. Sanitation consumes a fair number of the thirty-two steps required to make a good wine, and winemaker's joke that their first wine, when they did every step, was their best. After that, over-confidence lets them skip steps and the flavors go wrong in tiny ways that they hope no one notices.

Between modern science, stainless steel and technology, today's wines consistently turn out well, but premium wineries take that to the next level and here is how they do that. When they determine that the grapes have enough sugar for the yeast to produce the planned alcohol level, the team hand harvests the bunches at night, so they arrive at the winery by first light.

The grapes are washed and sorted to remove immature or spoiled fruit, leaves, twigs, and the occasional raccoon catching a ride and a snack in the bin. They love ripe grapes! The white grapes used for white wines are pressed immediately. Depending on the winemaker, they may be tossed in as whole bunches or de-stemmed first. That juice goes into a fermentation tank to begin the magic. Among premium wineries, concrete egg shaped fermenters are increasingly popular for white wines.

Most premium wines depend on the grape's native yeast for fermentation, which takes longer than commercially cultured yeast, but produces subtle, complex flavors. Big production wineries, on demanding timetables, prefer the aggressive, cultured yeast strains that work fast and can overcome problems caused by less than pristine grapes. Imagine wine yeast as a video game character with a big mouth, like Pac Man. As it consumes the yeast it excretes alcohol and that activity generates heat, so they cool the tanks to prevent the heat from destroying the flavors. The process releases carbon dioxide, which displaces oxygen, so wineries constantly run vent fans during the peak of fermentation. Although some wineries sidestep this problem by having their tanks outside.

When the alcohol level gets high enough, it kills the yeast, preferably very quickly, and fermentation stops. Winemakers need to avoid a long, drawn out death scene, like Hamlet, because the yeast will excrete toxic, headache producing types of alcohol. Winemakers have various tools to end fermentation fast. For example, they can lower the tank temperature, so the yeast goes dormant. When the yeast and sediment fall to the bottom, they pull the juice off the top, filtering it to remove the yeast, producing a clear, stable wine.

Red wine grapes are handled differently. They are de-stemmed and rigorously sorted because the juice and skin will be in contact during the fermentation. The more expensive the wine, the more grapes they discard, using mechanical and human sorters. They only want perfect grapes going into the fermentation tanks.

The tanks are sanitized, usually with tasteless ozone, and filled halfway to allow for the rising carbon dioxide bubbles. Pinot Noir tanks are wide and open topped, while Bordeaux varietals use an enclosed tank with a small hatch. Every surface the grapes or juice will touch is cleaned before and after.

When you talk with a winemaker, they'll say something like, "I've been with this winery for twelve harvests", because that experience helps them predict how the juice from each place will ferment. That transformation is not always a smooth process, so they have nutrients they can add to the juice to help the yeast be more effective. The carbon dioxide bubbles bring the skins to the surface, where they form a thick cap on the clear juice. Those skins contain the flavors and colors, so several times daily the winemakers 'punch down' the cap with a large paddle, infusing the juice with those components. Some wineries pump the juice from the bottom to the top, so it seeps down through the skins. Every step is scheduled and every action and measurement are recorded.

When the fermenting bubbles stop, the skins, seeds and expired yeast settle to the bottom. This mix is called the 'lees'. They remove the clear, 'free run' juice suspended above the lees, keeping that separate. Then they open the bottom hatch and put the remaining mix of juice and lees into the press. That juice is stored separately because the two lots have different flavors.

After fermentation, premium wines of both colors go into oak aging barrels, which soften the wine's sharp edges and compliment the flavors. Less expensive white wines are often kept in stainless tanks which makes them bright but a bit sharp. Sometimes winemakers decide to age a white wine in neutral oak barrels which doesn't add any flavor, but it gives them a softer mouth feel than the stainless steel.

Most premium white wines, like virtually every premium red wine, go into new and one-year old oak aging barrels. After six months the wines are 'racked', which means that the sediment has fallen to the bottom of the barrels, so the clear wine is removed through the top bung hole and put into a tank. The barrels are washed with ozone water and then refilled with wine for more aging. White wines are usually barrel aged for six to twelve months. Red wines are aged longer, the time determined by the thickness of the skins. Fragile Pinot Noir might require a year, while durable Cabernet Sauvignon needs from eighteen months to two years and sometimes more.

Eventually the barrels of clear, aged wine are transferred to a tank and allowed to settle, in preparation for bottling. White wines can be ready to sell in the coming year, but red wines normally need more time in the bottle to become appealing to the palate. And that is a simplified description of winemaking!

Answer F: Taste Buds & Tasting Notes

There are no 'standard' tasting notes. They range from very simple: wine name, year and price, to a deep dive into the wine's creation, vineyard location, harvest date, Brix number, barrel type, plus a sommelier-like description of the flavors to look for. Many people look at those kinds of flavor notes and think to themselves, "Gee, to me it just tastes like wine". We'll tell you a secret, to us, that's what it tastes like too!

Here is a Somm trick. One of their tools is the flavor wheel that lists the notes related to each varietal. While tasting the wine they run down that list. When their palates recognize a note, it's like a bell goes off in their head. Try it, it's cool when it happens to you!

About the Taste Buds

Your palate's flavor sensors are arranged in groups. Sweet, the flavor first liked by children, is on the tip of the tongue. That is because in nature, if it is sweet it is safe. That neural programming explains why the average American eats more than a hundred pounds of sugar yearly. Savory flavors are sensed on the wide, mid-tongue. These are predominantly composed of the alkaline minerals, calcium, magnesium, sodium and potassium, foundation nutrients that we consume quickly. Acids are sensed on the side of the tongue, which is important because wine has three acids: citric, malic and the grape's signature savory acid, tartaric. When a wine is harvested too late and lacks enough acid, it's called 'flabby'. There is no situation where that word is a compliment. Interesting note: the high acid levels in the Oregon and Washington State Pinots led to the development of a tulip top glass, designed to move the acidic wine to the sides away from the tongue's sensitive tip.

Because those three main wine flavors: sweet, savory and acidic, are tasted in the front half of the mouth, we can sniff, taste and spit the wine and still get an honest read without swallowing, although it is less fun. The two other major flavors the mouth detects, bitter and sour, are often associated with poisons and toxins. Bitter is sensed at the back of the tongue, and sour in the back corners.

Of course, there are nonpoisonous bitters and sours, but their acceptance depends on the body's experience with those foods. So, until a child realizes from experience that broccoli won't kill them, it won't taste good. That is why it's smart to expose your children to diverse flavors early, even if it isn't a primary part of the meal. Once they taste asparagus and realize that you are not trying to poison them, there is a better chance they'll develop a liking for it sooner.

Tasting Hint: when you hold the glass by the stem you are telling the host that you know something about wine. They will feel more comfortable sharing information and stories about the winery, and they may pour better vintages. On the other hand, if you're more comfortable holding it by the globe, go ahead. It's not like anyone is going to complain.

Answer G: Tasting Fees, Wine Clubs & Shipping

Wineries charge for tastings, but they may waive the fee for purchases or a new wine club membership. Members get a certain number of people included in a tasting session for free. For small wineries, the tasting room is their main venue for new sales, but the wine club is where they make their future. It is a discounted, subscription sales channel for their loyal customers.

The club members become their community, their circle of friends that they ship wine to several times a year, while inviting them to their special events. Some wine clubs create newsletters, member gifts and trips to foreign locales.

Thanks to the discount and the emotional connection, club members buy additional wines in between the scheduled shipments. If you like the wines and feel connected to the place, consider becoming a member. There is no fee to join, you can quit whenever you have too much wine, and the discounted pricing and shipping, along with getting access to their best products, is a good deal. Some wineries have cottages available for members to stay in for a small fee when they visit.

We feel that wine clubs awaken a part of our ancestral memory. Not that long ago most people farmed. In Europe, many people who grow up in the country, but move to the city for work, still fill their jugs at their local winery co-op during visits with their family. When they're back in the city, each night with dinner they drink the flavors of home. Being a wine club member connects us to a bucolic place that has a special spot in our terrestrial soul.

Should You Buy Wine at the Winery?

YES! Wine bottles are the best souvenirs, portable, storable, giftable, and later, when you enjoy them, it recalls the trip and gives you a great story to share over dinner. You can even stick a candle in the empty bottle to hold on to that memory. When you are at the wineries, you may see extra-large format bottles and think, 'What are those for?' Those are for the memory! They're purchased for events, during which the attendees sign the bottle with a metallic marker. Then the empty bottle is sent back to the winery to be re-corked, so the clients can display them and memorialize the event.

Here is the real reason to buy at the winery. The best wines are sold there. The widely distributed wines you buy in the stores are made from the least expensive grapes. You may find some great wines at restaurants because their buyers get them directly from the winery, and of course, dramatically mark them up. But the only other wines that measure up to those in the tasting room are the bottles in the wine club shipments or the cases you bring home with you.

Even the biggest wineries like Beringer, Mondavi, BV, etc., have a group of high quality, small production wines that they only pour and sell to the people who visit the tasting room. At some big wineries certain wines are only sold by the General Manager to special guests!

Most of the local wineries don't distribute, because this area sees so many visitors. So, if a wine appeals to you, buy it then and there, because you are not going to find it anyplace else.

Also, they only make a limited of cases, so they may not have it later on. If you're buying more than a few bottles, the wineries can usually ship them to you. In fact, the small wineries are the easiest places to buy, because the big wineries have the most shipping restrictions, due to their distributor agreements. But, you can buy the wine and ship it yourself, although you will need to address to someplace where a person will sign for the box because it is alcohol.

If you're assembling bottles from numerous wineries, use a local shipper. If you are pressed for time your hotel can likely arrange for a pick up. If you are not staying in a full-service hotel, there will be a storefront shipper nearby. In the hot weather they time the shipments to avoid heat damaging the precious wine. If you buy wine in August, you may have to wait until October or November for them to ship. Another solution is to take it with you on the plane as checked luggage. Simply buy an inexpensive, wine shipping box (they come in twos, sixes and twelves), tape and a marker at a shipping store and bring it to the airport.

That way your wine arrives home with you with less potential for heat damage and it is an economic solution. Traveling wine luggage is also a solution and some of the wineries sell them in their gift area. A filled six pack weighs about twenty pounds, and a twelve pack weighs forty pounds. If handling the weight and bulk of a twelve pack is an issue, then get couple of six packs and make sure you mark the box as "Fragile Glass' in big letters.

In many cases, taking it with you as luggage will be cheaper than having it shipped. After you get the wine home, let the bottles sit for a week to get over the bottle shock of shipping before you begin enjoying them. And watch the movie "Bottle Shock" again. Much of it was filmed in Calistoga and downtown Sonoma so see if you can pick out the locations!

Overview of the Southern Wine Country

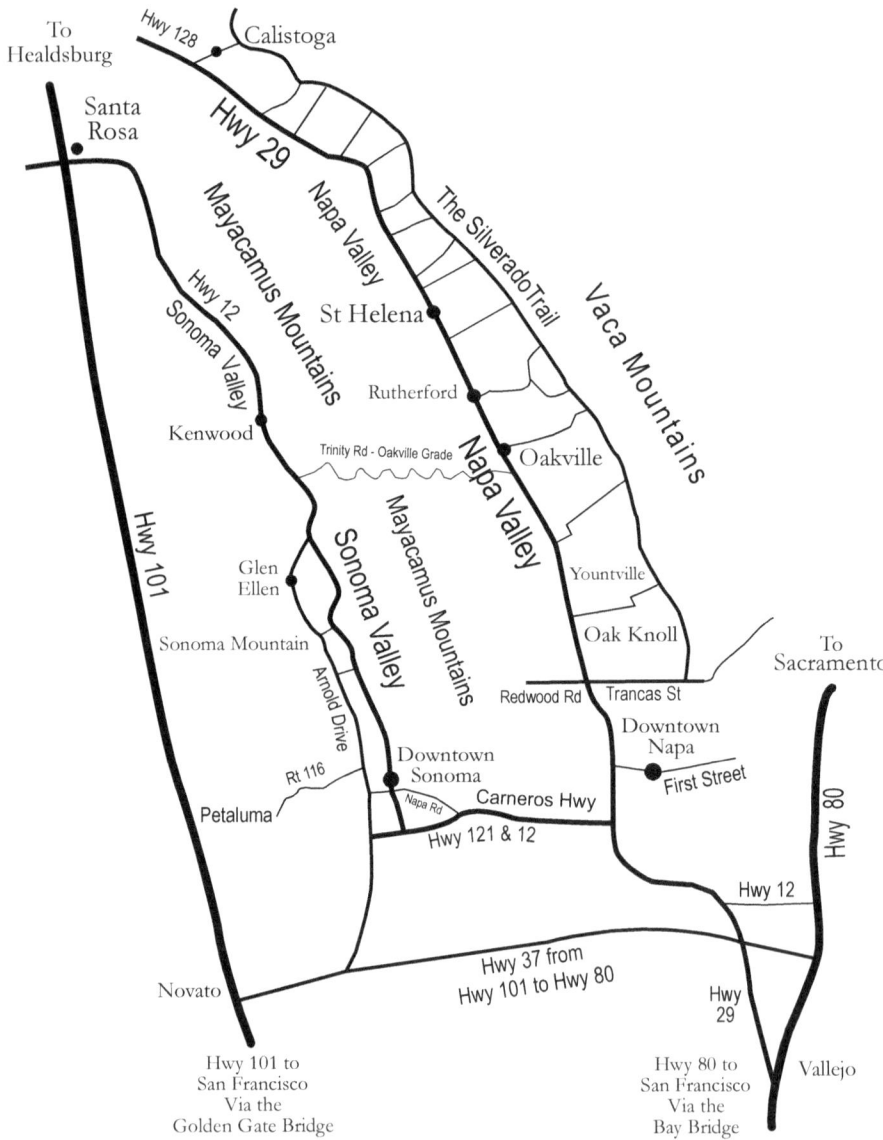

Using the Directory & the Maps

Because wineries are private businesses, when they change owners, teams, phone numbers, websites or run out of wine they rarely contact us. So, you use this directory as a guide, not the final authority. The listing includes the winery's name, a short descriptive phrase, primary wines, contact information, hours, any comments about what makes them special and a letter reference to the Maps at the back if the winery appears on one. We have listed about three hundred wineries, of the approximately six hundred in Sonoma. Why do we leave so many out? Because most wineries do not see guests, and some only welcome visitors if they are wine club members or previous buyers. So, while this is not a comprehensive winery list, it is suited to a travel book! Be aware that while the downtown tasting rooms often have great wines, they move more often than the wineries so consult their websites.

About the Grape Varietals

We list a winery's grape varietals because those rarely change. We often describe them as Bordeaux or Burgundy, the places of those grape varietal's recent origins. The red Bordeaux grapes are Cabernet Sauvignon, Merlot, Cabernet Franc, Malbec and

Petite Verdot. The white Bordeaux grapes are Sauvignon Blanc and the less common Semillon. The Burgundy grapes are the white Chardonnay and the red Pinot Noir. These two groups are the most popular. Occasionally wineries also use Rhone, Spanish and Italian style grapes and we note that.

About the Hours

This is farm country so tasting rooms are open in the daytime, from about 10am to 5pm. Many wineries are by appointment due to staffing constraints, but some of the biggest are open to walk-in visitors, so check their websites. When we write 'Collector' in the listing, those wineries expect their visitors to be interested in purchasing wine at their price point, or becoming members in the club. These 'collector' wineries often make their money solely from selling wine, so they primarily host wine club members. They may resist scheduling a tasting unless there is a good prospect for a sale or a new member. That does not mean that you must buy. What if you don't like the wine? But before you visit, know their prices and bring a credit card. In comparison, the big wineries see more traffic and also make money from their tasting fees, tours, seminars and events so whether or not you buy wine is less of an issue.

Fires

The fires that periodically besiege the North Bay Wine Country from the late Summer until November, when it rains, leaves scars that last for two to five years, until the foliage recovers. While many of the plants are flame resistant, some buildings are not, so we note when a winery was damaged by fires. Depending on numerous factors, the winery can rebound quickly, or be in for an extended comeback. Fortunately, the vineyards serve as fire breaks so while that year's grapes may, or may not suffer from smoke taint, the vines survive, and they are the heart of a winery's life. Because the weather here is mild year-round, many visitors now come in the Winter and Spring as a way to not have their plans disrupted by smoke.

The Maps

All the maps are listed on page 4, and the Directory Maps at the back of the book are also marked with a large, easy to read letter that connects to the winery listings. The maps in the earlier part of the book provide an overview while the Directory Maps highlight the growing regions. Why do we need maps in the age of GPS? Because our maps show you what other wineries are near your destination and more importantly, they can help you plot a safer routes by emphasizing right-hand turns. GPS will show you the shorter route, but not necessarily the safest.

This is is important because both Napa and Sonoma are served mostly by narrow, two-lane roads with few traffic lights, and on most days a high proportion of the drivers have been drinking. Right-hand turns are safer for everyone. Wine Country has twice the state's average number of 'Driving Under the Influence' arrests, plus plenty of accidents. But it is rare to see a crash that happened when someone was making a right-hand turn. The only left turns you should make are at intersections with light traffic, great visibility, or traffic lights.

Avoid driving on the valley's unlit back roads at night, especially when inebriated, because even the locals occasionally run into ditches on those country routes. In Sonoma that means staying on better lit highways as much as possible.

Allow Extra Time

When planning your trips, allow *at least* an extra ten minutes, for getting your partially inebriated group into and out of the car, as well as walking to and from the winery, which is often a long ways. Finding your way also requires extra time because the street and winery signs are often not obvious. Winery signs are hard to spot at fifty miles an hour, and some only have addresses on mailboxes. Even professional guides, who are not drinking and know the area miss the entrances now and then.

Wine Country crossroads are marked with signs about one hundred feet before the turn. Sometimes the sign is across the road from the intersection, on a foliage obscured pole. When you see the sign, start slowing down and watch the painted lines on the asphalt as your indicators. Late in the season the paint fades and bushes lean into the roads, so drive slower and pay attention! It is important to plan your time well so that you don't need to rush, and you can enjoy the scenery safely!

The Winery Directory

A. Rafanelli Winery – A Popular Dry Creek Winery – Wines: Cabernet Sauvignon, Merlot, Zinfandel – 4685 W. Dry Creek Rd. Healdsburg CA 95448 – Dry Creek Valley – www.arafanelliwinery.com – (707) 433-1385 – (parties over 6) cash/check only – Hours: 10:00am to 4:00pm – Appointment – No Tours – This is a popular winery, and they enjoy tremendous loyalty from their customers. The casual tasting is done in the barrel room or outside in the garden and often by a family member. There is a gate at the bottom of the driveway. Navigation: They are located on the left side of the road just north of Lambert Bridge Road. Map F

Abbot's Passage & Mercantile – Sonoma Valley – Wines: Rhone Varietals and Blends – 777 Madrone Road, Glen Ellen, CA 95442 – www.abbotspassage.com – (707) 939-3017 – Hours: 11:00pm to 5:00pm Thursdays – Monday – info@abbotspassage.com. This big, rambling winery five miles north of the Plaza is one of the more historic parts of California's Wine Country. The land surrounding the winery has been planted to vineyards since 1860. There is a 400-year-old Bay tree out behind the winery. They have a spacious, comfortable culinary tasting, with a lovely gift section focused on products from women owned businesses. The wines are well made. They are just one minute off of Route 12 on Madrone Road, which is a traffic light with Hamel Winery on the right. Map D

Acorn Winery – South Eastern Russian River – Field Blends – Wines: Sangiovese, Dolcetto, Cabernet Franc, Zinfandel, Syrah, Blends – 12040 Old Redwood Highway. Healdsburg CA 95448 www.acornwinery.com – (707) 433-6440 – Hours: Appointment – The property was first planted to grapes in the 1850's. They produce some field blends, a traditional method where the numerous varietals are planted together and then combined in the tanks. They are located down a long, narrow drive, leading to an odd collection of buildings, and a partially open–air tasting room. They have a loyal following and well–made wines. Their sign is located north of the drive for Rodney Strong and the J Winery on the opposite (east) side of the road. The sign is not large, so take your time as you get close. Map E

Adobe Road Winery – Tasting Room on the Petaluma River Front – Wines: Cabernet Franc, Cabernet Sauvignon, Meritage, Petite Syrah, Pinot Noir, Sauvignon Blanc, Syrah, Zinfandel, Port – 6 Petaluma Blvd North Suite A1 in the Great Petaluma Mill, Petaluma, CA – www.adoberoadwines.com – (707) 774-6699 – Hours: 11:00am to 7:00pm – This long time Petaluma winery opened a tasting room in their downtown for their wonderful wines. It is owned by the sports car racer, Kevin Buckler. The winery is in the nearby corporate park, along with some of his race cars.

Alexander Valley Vineyards – Charming Old Style Sonoma – Wines: Gewürztraminer, Chardonnay, Viognier, Pinot Noir, Sangiovese, Zinfandel, Merlot, Cabernet Sauvignon – 8644 Highway 128 Healdsburg CA 95448 – www.avvwine.com – (707) 433-7209 – Hours: 10:00am – 5:00pm – Cave Tours – Wine and Cheese Pairings This is a friendly winery with a great staff, a cute gift shop and some good wines and they do reserve tastings and a vineyard hike by appointment. It has that wonderfully inclusive feeling that we love about Northern Sonoma. They have caves, which makes sense, since they are tucked up against a hillside in the southern part of the Alexander Valley, close to the Hanna winery. They have a nice variety of wines that are moderately priced. Map G

Amista Vineyards – Dry Creek Charm – Wines: Chardonnay, Rose of Syrah, Syrah, Zinfandel, Cabernet Sauvignon – 3320 Dry Creek Road Healdsburg CA 95448 – www.amistavineyards.com – (707) 431-9200 – Hours: 11:00am – 4:30pm – Their 'barn' is surrounded by 20 acres of their own Chardonnay and Syrah vines on the gravel rich floor of the Dry Creek Valley. Their Zinfandel and Cabernet Sauvignon grapes come from local growers. The tasting room is spacious with great views of the vineyards outside and a relaxed, friendly style. Map F

Amapola Creek Vineyards and Winery – Sonoma Valley Hillside – Wines: Cabernet Sauvignon – 392 London Way, Sonoma, CA 95476 – www.amapolacreek.com – (707) 938-3783 – Hours: 10:00am to 3:00pm Thursday – Monday – The home winery of Richard Arrowood, an iconic winemaker working exclusively in Sonoma County for more than for 50+ years, but reportedly retiring. From 1974 through 1990, he created the wines for Chateau St. Jean, where he developed some of the first vineyard–designate Chardonnay and Cabernet Sauvignon produced in Sonoma County. Map D

Amphora Winery – Dry Creek Valley at the Timber Creek Center – Wines: Petite Syrah, Zinfandel, Pinot Noir, Merlot, Cabernet Sauvignon, Syrah, Chardonnay – 4791 Dry Creek Rd. Bldg. 6 Healdsburg CA 95448 – www.amphorawines.com – (707) 431-7767 – Hours: 11:00am to 4:30pm – Groups by Appointment – This is a wonderful little winery located in a big white building just a short walk from Papapietro–Perry, Peterson and Kokomo. The winemaker was previously a potter and the tasting room also serves as a gallery. During harvest, women visitors can sometimes crush grapes with their feet, Lucy style. Those

'Lucy' wine proceeds benefit a charity. This is a fun winery to visit, a good value and the winemaker/owner is often around, if not pouring. Map F

Anaba Wines – Los Carneros on the Main Road – Wines: Chardonnay, Pinot Noir, Viognier, Rhone style blends – 60 Bonneau St. Sonoma CA 95476 – (707) 996-4188 – Hours: 11:00am–5:00pm – As you come up from San Francisco over the Golden Gate Bridge, Anaba is among the first dozen wineries you encounter in Los Carneros. They are at the intersection with the flashing light north of the Racetrack and just past the gas station. Turn left there and then right into their parking lot. Their winery and vineyards are behind the tasting room which is cute, comfortable, welcoming and surprisingly quiet despite being at a busy intersection. They make good wines. Map B

Annadel Estate Winery – Sonoma Valley Boutique – Wines: Bordeaux and Burgundy Blends, General French – 6687 Sonoma Highway, Santa Rosa, CA 95409 – www.annadelestatewinery.com – (707) 537-8007 – Hours: 11:00am–5:00pm – Appointment – This pretty, bucolic winery is owned and operated by two sommeliers. It sits on a property dating back to the 1880's. They also have five acres devoted to flowers and they host small weddings and events. Map D

Arista Winery – Russian River at the Edge of Dry Creek – Wines: Pinot Noir, Chardonnay – 7015 Westside Rd. Healdsburg CA 95448 – www.aristawinery.com – (707) 473-0606 – Hours: 11:00am–5:00pm Appointment – This is a small, pretty winery tucked in the western hillsides south of the town of Healdsburg. They have an intimate tasting room, surrounded by comfortable tables that are nested in the gardens, built around huge boulders, with a distinctly Zen feeling. There is a great place to picnic under the trees by prearrangement. The tasting is pleasant, and the staff is relaxed and friendly. The wines, over the years have moved into the upper premium region. Map E

Armida Winery – At the Edge of Russian River and Dry Creek Valleys with Great Views – Wines: Rosé, Pinot Noir, Chardonnay, Zinfandel, Gewürztraminer, Sauvignon Blanc, Cabernet Sauvignon – 2201 Westside Rd. Healdsburg CA 95448 – www.armidawinery.com – (707) 433-2222 – Hours: 11:00am–5:00pm – The Geodesic Dome winery sits on top of a hill with great views of the Russian River Valley. The tasting room is bright and spacious with some interesting gifts and the staff is friendly. There are gardens, patios and picnic areas. The wine list includes a nice variety, reasonably priced in a part of the valley that has become increasingly expensive. Map E

Arrowood Vineyards – Sonoma Valley – Shares a driveway with the Imagery Winery – Wines: Chardonnay, Pinot Blanc, Viognier, Gewürztraminer, Merlot, Cabernet Sauvignon, Syrah, Riesling – 14347 Sonoma Highway. Glen Ellen CA 95442 – www.arrowoodwinery.com – (707) 935-2600 – Hours: 10:00am to 4:30pm – This is a pretty property and a charming tasting room just six miles north of the Sonoma Plaza. They have nice outdoor patios and a good gift shop, although the tastings have always been done inside. The winery is surrounded by its vineyards. The staff is knowledgeable and friendly. They are owned by the Jackson Family. Map D

Auteur – Sonoma Plaza – Wines: Bordeaux and Burgundy – 373 1st St. West, Sonoma, CA 95476 – www.auteurwines.com – (707)–938-9211 Hours: 10:00am to 5:30pm Appointment – This is a premium tasting room by appointment just steps off the Sonoma Plaza. This is part of a growing community of high-end producers of small lot wines that are choosing to locate in the convenient downtown, rather than deal with the complications of setting up their tasting room at a winery or vineyard. Three Sticks Winery is just around the corner. Map A

B Wise Vineyards – Sonoma Valley with Two Locations – Wines: Bordeaux and Burgundy Blends – 9077 Sonoma Highway. Kenwood CA 95452 – www.bwisevineyards.com – 707-282-9169

– Hours: 10:30am to 4:30pm – lounge@bwisevineyards.com – This is a high-end winery in the mid-Sonoma Valley with two locations, a tasting room on Highway 29 and a small cave built into the eastern hillsides near their home and offices. Map D

B.R. Cohn Winery – Sonoma Valley with Grapevines, Olives and Music – Wines: Cabernet Sauvignon, Zinfandel, Chardonnay, Merlot, Syrah – 15000 Sonoma Highway Glen Ellen CA 95442 – www.brcohn.com (707) 938-4064 – Hours: 10:00am to 5:00pm – Tours by Appointment – This is five miles north of the Plaza on a picture-perfect hillside, surrounded by vines and olive groves. The building was once a stagecoach stop for the Sonoma to Santa Rosa run, that was transformed into a home by Bruce Cohn, a native of this area, and the manager of the Doobie Brothers. Later, as the winery expanded, it became the tasting room for the winery outback. They have both inside and outside tasting areas, a separate gift shop for their olive oils and related products, and picnic tables. Behind the winery is a large event space, that is coupled with a spot in the vineyards to accommodate weddings. During the summer they also host concerts, that have continued even though the Cohn family no longer owns the property. Map D

Bacchus – South Healdsburg – Wines: A varety from several wineries – 14210 Bacchus Landing Way, Healdsburg, CA 95448 – www.bacchuslanding.com – (707) 799-1821 – Hours: 10:00am to 5:00pm – Opened in 2021 this is a large space that hosts about five winery tasting rooms with inside and outside spaces off Westside Road by downtown Healdsburg. Map E

Bacigalupi Vineyards – Russian River Valley on Westside Road – Wines: Burgundy Blends, General French – 4353 Westside Road Healdsburg, CA 95448 – www.bacigalupivineyards.com – (707) 473-0115 – Hours: 11:00am to 4:30pm – tastingroom@bacigalupivineyards.com – This is a small, friendly hospitality building tucked just off Westside Road, in a hollow below their revered vineyards. Why are they revered? Because they were one of the main sources for the chardonnay grapes that went into the Chateau Montelena Chardonnay that won at the 1976 Judgment of Paris. There is a great photo showing Grandma Bacigalupi standing with the winemaker Mike Grgich, next to the tall vines. When we first started visiting this tasting room, hosted by the family, the original vines were still there, although the vineyard had since been replanted. One of the great ironies in wine country is that while it was two Napa wineries that won at that famous wine tasting, the grapes for the Chardonnay were mostly from their sister county Sonoma. Map E

Balletto Vineyards – Southern Russian River Valley Outside Sebastopol – Cozy Tasting Room – Wines: Chardonnay, Pinot Grigio, Pinot Gris, Pinot Noir, Rosé of Pinot Noir, Syrah. Gewürztraminer, Zinfandel – 5700 Occidental Rd. Santa Rosa CA 95401 – www.ballettovineyards.com – (707) 568-2455 – Hours: 10:00am–5:00pm Appointment – Balleto has numerous vineyards in this part of the southern Russian River Valley. They are located down a long gravel road in a pretty, flat part of the valley between Santa Rosa and Sebastopol. The winery is a steel warehouse building surrounded by vines, but they have a pretty outdoor sitting area, and the tasting room is cute and cozy, with some nice gifts and a friendly staff. The experience is relaxed, and the wines are good and true to the area. Map E

Bartholomew Park Winery – Southern Sonoma Valley east of the Plaza with a Park – Wines: Sauvignon Blanc, Merlot, Syrah, Zinfandel, Cabernet Sauvignon – 1000 Vineyard Lane Sonoma CA 95476 – www.bartpark.com – (707) 935-9511 – Hours: 11:00am to 4:30pm – They are located just to the east of downtown Sonoma and it includes a lovely picnic grounds. Around 2020 the winery changed owners and the entire experience went through a dramatic upgrade and now tastings are offered inside and out on a lovely oak knoll. Allow time to visit the gallery, it is a wonderful space to enjoy art. This building has a long history, including being the local hospital, and a home for wayward women sent from San Francisco, which of course caused all kinds of chaos for the locals. The original property, owned by the Bartholomew family was deeded for the public good many years ago as a park, and the winery and vineyards are residents. The next property over is Buena Vista, one of California's most historic wineries, so you can combine the two into a very convenient day. Map B

Battaglini Estate Winery – Southern Russian River Near Olivet Road – Wines: Zinfandel, Chardonnay, Petite Sirah – 2948 Piner Road, Santa Rosa, CA 95401 – www.battagliniwines.com – (707) 318-8944 – Hours: 10:00am to 5:00pm Appointment – This is very much a small family winery, producing about 2500 cases of good wine, on land that has been farmed to grapes since the late 1800's. There is an Italian style to the place and a homey feel. This area has been known for growing great Zinfandel since grape growing began here. They are nearby DeLoach, Inman Family and Harvest Moon. Map E

Bella Wine Caves – Northwestern Dry Creek Valley – Wines: Zinfandel, Syrah – 9711 W. Dry Creek Road. CA 95448 – www.BellaWinery.com – (707) 473-9171 – Hours: 11:00am to 4:30pm – This is a small, charming family–run winery located up a narrow road at the top of the Dry Creek Valley. The tasting is in their caves that are dug into the hillsides beneath their vineyards. Whenever there is a special weekend, such as the Barrel Tasting or Passport, this is always a favorite stop for those in the know. It is pet friendly and has accessible picnic tables on the lawn with wonderful views of the valley. The caves are especially nice on a hot day. Map F

Beltane Ranch – Sonoma Valley with an Historic B&B – Wines: Sauvignon Blanc and Zinfandel – 11775 Sonoma Highway, Glen Ellen, CA 95442 – www.beltaneranch.com – (707) 833-4233 – Hours: Appointment – This is a B&B at a House built in 1892 on a 105 Acres that sells wines from their vineyards. The site was the home of Mary Ellen Johnson. an important Abolitionist and one San Francisco's wealthiest women. Map D

Bennett Valley Cellars – Sonoma Plaza tasting room – Wines: Bordeaux and Burgundy Blends – 127 E Napa St, Sonoma, CA 95476 – www.bennettvalleycellars.com – (707) 934-8173 – Hours: 12:00pm – 6:00pm. Map A

Benovia Winery – Southern Russian River – Wines: Pinot Noir, Chardonnay – 3339 Hartman Road Santa Rosa, CA 95401 – www.benoviawinery.com – (707) 921-1040 – Hours: 10:00am to 3:30pm Appointment – This is a charming, family run winery surrounded by their vines just east of Olivet Lane, nearby De-Loach and Inman Family. They see limited numbers of guests by appointment. Map E

Benziger Family Winery – Sonoma Valley Biodynamic Advocates & Tram Tours – Wines: Sauvignon Blanc, Chardonnay, Pinot Noir, Cabernet Sauvignon, Merlot, Syrah, Muscat, Port. 1883 London Ranch Rd. Glen Ellen CA 95442 – www.benziger.com – (707) 935-4527 – This is one of the great wineries of the Sonoma Valley, Biodynamic/Organic, Caves, Gardens, Gifts, picnic tables, and the best tours in Sonoma. A tractor pulls passenger laden trams up into the Biodynamic Vineyards for a great lecture, followed by tours of the caves and the winery. Tours run on the 1/2 hour, starting at 11, except 12:30, until 3. They have added a Partner's Tour that goes more deeply into the vineyards and their approach to agriculture. Map D

Bonneau Wines – Los Carneros on the Main Road at the Carneros Deli – Wines: Cabernet Sauvignon, Zinfandel, Chardonnay, Malbec, Petite Syrah, Meritage – 23001 Arnold Drive, Sonoma CA 95476 www.bonneauwine.com – (800) 996-0420 – Hours: 11:00am–6:00pm – The Bonneau family came from Bordeaux in the 1920's and has farmed this land since then. Since the 1990s, they have been selling grapes to other wineries. In 2002, they introduced their own wines and they also source grapes from some of the area's best vineyards. It helps to know the right people. It is a low-key location, the tasting room is attached to their deli so get a snack at the same time. Map B

Buena Vista Winery – Sonoma Valley East of the Plaza with History – Wines: Pinot Gris, Chardonnay, Pinot Noir, Merlot, Syrah, Port – 18000 Old Winery Rd. Sonoma CA 95476 – www.BuenaVistaCarneros.com – (800) 926-1266 – (707) 265-1472 – Hours: 10:00am to 5:00pm – This is California's most historic winery, founded in 1857 just minutes from the old town of Sonoma. The fragrant Eucalyptus trees that line the winding road lead you there. It is an extraordinary property and the original buildings have been beautifully restored. There are historic tours, special tastings and tons of education. The winery has wooden production tanks on the main floor and a tool library on the top floor. The restoration of the main winery was an amazing project and the place is unique. Map B

Cast Winery – Northern Dry Creek Valley – Bordeaux, Burgundy Blends, Zinfandel, Petite Sirah – 8500 Dry Creek Road Geyserville CA 95441 – Wines: – www.castwines.com – (707) 431-1225 – Hours: 10:00am to 5:00pm – Appointment – A small family-owned winery in an especially pretty part of the valley just south of Ferrari Carano. Map F

Chalk Hill Estate Winery – North Eastern Russian River South of Alexander Valley in the Chalk Hill District – Beautiful Setting – Wines: Chardonnay, Sauvignon Blanc, Pinot Gris, Cabernet Sauvignon, Merlot, Semillon, Blends – 10300 Chalk Hill Rd. Healdsburg CA 95448 – www.chalkhill.com – (707) 838-4306 – Hours: 10:00am–4:00pm This is a stately winery in a gorgeous location that makes wonderful wines. The building is grand and the tasting is excellent. The Chalk Hill section is known for its white, rocky soil, which you can see jutting out of the cuts along the roads. This is a great place to bring your camera. Map E

Chateau Saint Jean Winery – Queen of the Sonoma Valley – Wines: Pinot Blanc, Chardonnay, Viognier, Pinot Noir, Merlot, Malbec, Cabernet Sauvignon – 8555 Sonoma Highway, Kenwood CA 95452 – www.chateaustjean.com – (707) 833-4134

Hours: 10:00am–5:00pm – This is a Sonoma Valley favorite because of the great architecture, gardens, gift shop, deli/market and tours. They have two tasting rooms, the regular and the reserve in the wood lined mansion. The staff is friendly and knowledgeable. It is a popular, well distributed label that you'll find easily when you get home. The property was owned originally by a couple from Michigan, and they created a pond next to the mansion in the shape of the Great Lakes with Michigan in the center. Over time, the pond broke down and now that's been replaced with a patio, filled with comfortable table seating. The main tasting room is where you will also find the deli and restrooms. The Mansion Reserve Tasting room also has outdoor seating by request. It is a elegant experience. Map D

Christopher Creek Winery – Southern Russian River Valley – Family Grape Growers – 641 Limerick Lane Healdsburg CA 95448 – www.christophercreek.com – (707) 433-2001 – Hours: 11:00am–5:00pm Appointment – The Wasserman family has been growing grapes and other types of fruit in this section of the Russian River Valley for many years and they give much of the credit for their excellent wines to the quality of their grapes. It is a charming winery, a small tasting room, relaxed and friendly with lovely views of the hills. Map E

Cline Cellars – Los Carneros just off the Main Road – History and Diversity – Wines: Mourvèdre, Carignane, Syrah, Zinfandel, Viognier, Marsanne, Roussanne, Blends – 24737 Arnold Dr. Sonoma CA 95476 – www.clinecellars.com – (707) 940-4000 – Hours: 10:00am–6:00pm – Tours – This was the original site of the San Francisco Solano mission, the 21st and final Mission established in California. Later the mission was moved to the Sonoma Plaza. It is a great location, and the grounds are expansive and park–like. They do tours and have a bird and animal collection. They built a charming museum for antique scale models of the 21 Franciscan Missions. The tasting room is homey and friendly, and popular, especially late in the day, because they are on the right side of the road as people are leaving the valleys to return to the city. The wines are always good, and they make a wide variety. Fred Cline was one of the first people in the area to use sheep for grazing as part of their vineyard management which is not only 'Green' but cute. The winery is run on solar and there is an educational display about that. The buildings make you feel like you're at a country farm. Map B

Clos Du Bois Wines – CLOSED AS OF 2021 – Alexander Valley – 19410 Geyserville Ave. Geyserville CA 95441 – Map G

Colagrossi Wines – Downtown Windsor – Wines: Specializing in Italian Varietals – 7755 Bell Road Windsor CA – www.colagrossiwines.com – (707) 529-5459 – Hours: Appointment – They produce 1000 cases of wines yearly, made by the owner.

Collier Falls Vineyard – Dry Creek Valley – Wines: Bordeaux and Burgundy Blends, Zinfandel, Petite Sirah – 4791 Dry Creek Road, Bldg 11 Healdsburg , CA 95448 – www.collierfalls.com – (707) 433-0100 Hours: Appointment – This is a wonderful couple who started it in the late 1990's and produces wines from their own twenty acres. Check with them about where they are currently offering tastings. Map F

Comstock Wines – Dry Creek Valley – Wines: Bordeaux, Burgundy, Zinfandel, Grenache, General French – 1290 Dry Creek Road Healdsburg, CA 95448 – www.comstockwines.com – (707) 723-3011 – Hours: 10:30am to 4:30pm – A spacious winery with a lovely terrace overlooking their Merlot vineyards on the valley floor, convenient to downtown Healdsburg. Map F

Copain – Russian River Valley on Eastside Road south of Healdsburg – Wines: Pinot Noir, Chardonnay, Syrah, Picpoul, Trousseau – 7800 Eastside Road Healdsburg, CA 95448 – www.copainwines.com – (707) 837-8822 – Hours: 12:00am to 3:00pm – Appointment – A small ultra-premium producer on the east side of the Russian River in an area with very few wineries. It is a lovely location and a gracious experience. Map E

Coturri Winery – Western Sonoma Valley – Wines: Very interesting Blends, General French – 6725 Enterprise Road Glen Ellen, CA 95442 – www.coturriwinery.com – Hours: Appointment – tony@coturriwinery.com – the Coturri family are well-known as organic growers who manage numerous other properties besides their own. Their own wines are unique blends which includes an apple cider. They are tucked away in the rolling hills to the west of the Sonoma Valley and Glen Ellen and south of Bennett Valley Road. Map D

D' Argenzio – Santa Rosa Office Park Location – Wines: A very wide variety with a focus on Italian varietals – 1301 Cleveland Ave Suite D, Santa Rosa, CA 95401 – www.dargenziowine.com – (707) 546-2466 Hours: Monday – Tuesday Appointment, Wednesday, Thursday, and Sunday 11:00am–5:00pm, Friday–Saturday 11:00am to 7:00pm – reservations@dargenziowine.com – D'Argenzio Winery is owned and operated by Ray and Ricci D'Argenzio (twin brothers) with Ray's daughter, Breanna Tamburin, running the Santa Rosa wine tasting room. They offer wine tastings, tours, antipasti boards, wood–fired pizza, bocce ball, a patio area, and they hosts numerous special events.

Dane Cellars – Sonoma Valley South of Sonoma Plaza – Wines: Chenin Blanc, Zinfandel, Cabernet Sauvignon – P.O. Box 555 Vineburg CA. 95487 – www.danecellars.com – (707)–529-5856 – Hours: Appointment – bart@danecellars.com – This is a very small family winery producing excellent wines from an industry veteran.

David Coffaro Vineyard and Winery – Dry Creek Valley – Intimate and Innovative – Wines: Pinot Noir, Cabernet Sauvignon, Petite Syrah, Carignane, Zinfandel, Estate Cuvee – 7485 Dry Creek Rd. Geyserville CA 95441 – www.coffaro.com – (707) 433-9715 – Hours: 11:00am–4:00pm – This is a family run winery by a long time local producer. You taste in the barrel room. They were one of the first producers locally to offer futures for sale. Map F

Davis Family Vineyards – Healdsburg at Front Street – Wines: Chardonnay, Syrah, Zinfandel, Cabernet Sauvignon, Pinot Noir, Apple Brandy, Olive Oil – 52 Front Street, Healdsburg CA 95448 – www.davisfamilyvineyards.com – (707) 433-3858 – Hours: 11:00am–4:00pm Thursday – Sunday – This winery produces a wide variety of wines, both from their own ridge top vineyards in the Russian River Valley, and from grapes sourced in the area, most notably Dutton Estates, a collection of vineyards spread around the southern side of the river. While they have a fair number of their own Zinfandel vines planted in the late 1800's, it is their younger Pinot and Syrah that standout and win the gold medals. The tasting/barrel room is one of the longest lasting Front Street Wineries in an eclectic commercial area beside the Russian River. It is charming experience and they have an outdoor patio next to the flowing water. Map H

De La Montanya – Dry Creek – Wines: Diverse – 999 Foreman Lane Healdsburg CA 95448 – www.dlmwine.com – (707) 433-3711 – Hours: 11:00am–4:30pm – This is a good winery with a fun approach. They are a little tricky to find because the turn off West Dry Creek Road onto Foreman Lane snakes around and goes under the road to get to the winery. They have a small tasting room and pretty grounds and they do nice events, but they have limited hours. Map F

De Loach Vineyards – Southern Russian River on Olivet Lane – Wines: Sauvignon Blanc, Chardonnay, Pinot Noir, Zinfandel – 1791 Olivet Rd. Santa Rosa CA 95401 – www.deloachvineyards.com – (707) 526-9111 – Hours: 10:00am–4:30pm – Appointments strongly suggested – This is the largest of the Olivet Lane wineries. They are Biodynamic/Organic and have a cool education demonstration garden. The tasting is in a separate hospitality house behind the winery with a large patio area and very comfortable indoor seating. It makes you feel like you are inside of a beautifully decorated private home. There is a separate picnic area. They make great wines that they offer in a gracious setting. Map E

De Lorimier Winery – Alexander Valley making Big Reds – Wines: Meritage, Malbec, Chardonnay, Sauvignon Blanc and Zinfandel – 2001 Highway. 128 Geyserville CA 95441 – www.delorimierwinery.com – (707) 857–2000 – Hours: 10:30am – 5:00pm – Now owned by the Wilsons, who have numerous wineries in northern Sonoma, they are focusing on single vineyard designated Cabernets. Their vineyards also provide grapes for their various other wines. Map G

Deerfield Ranch Winery – Sonoma Valley Cave Tasting – Wines: Blends, Meritage, Cab, Chardonnay, Dessert Wine, Merlot, Pinot Noir, Sangiovese, Sauvignon Blanc, Syrah – 10200 Sonoma Highway Kenwood CA 95442 – www.deerfieldranch.com – (707) 833-5215 – Hours: 10:30–4:30pm – They had a long road making their winery accessible to the public due to county regulations, but some wonderful wines come out of their caves. This is a high quality organic winery obsessed with clean, healthy wines that they pour in their charming caves. To reach the tasting area, you walk through their outside winery, which is jammed packed with tanks, sorters and presses, and the whole experience is remarkable. Map D

Deux Amis Winery see Zouzounis Wines

D and L Carinalli Vineyards – Sebastopol – Wines: Chardonnay, Pinot Noir, Pinot Grigio and Vin Rosé wines – 2900 Llano Road Santa Rosa, CA 95407 – www.dlcarinallivineyards.com – (707) 795-7052 – Hours: Appointment – A very small, but excellent family winery with no tasting room, but willing to do tastings by appointment.

Donum Estate – Los Carneros Sculpture Park and Winery – Wines: Pinot Noir, Chardonnay, Rose – 24500 Ramal Road Sonoma, CA 95476 – www.thedonumestate.com – (707) 939-2290 – Hours: 10:00am–5:00pm Appointment – This very fine producer was transformed in order to host impressive modern sculpture from the owner's collection. The wines are excellent, and the sculpture tour is wonderful. The location on the rolling hills of Los Carneros can be cool early in the day and windy and sun soaked later, so dress accordingly for the tour, although the tasting is in their very unique tasting building. Map C

Dry Creek Vineyard – At the Center of the Valley – A Fun Experience – Wines: Chenin Blanc, Fumé Blanc, Zinfandel, Merlot, Cabernet Sauvignon, Meritage – 3770 Lambert Bridge Rd. Healdsburg CA 95448 – www.drycreekvineyard.com – (707) 433-1000 – Hours: 10:30am to 4:30pm – They are located near the Dry Creek Store and across from Passalacqua. Their photo gallery shows many of the celebrity events at which their wines have been poured. Not bad for an up–valley winery! They were one of the first modern wineries in the area and they continue to produce wonderful products. They have a nice picnic area shielded from the road, and the staff is friendly and relaxed. There is a small gift area and they do neat events. Map F

Dunstan Wines – Sonoma Valley West of the Plaza – Wines: Rose, Pinot Noir, Chardonnay – 1945 Felder Road Sonoma, CA 95476 – www.dunstanwines.com – (707) 933-3839 Hours: 10:00am to 3:00pm Wednesday – Sunday – Appointment – orders@dunstanwines.com – The Durell Vineyards sit on the western hills abeam downtown Sonoma. This is a premium producer that appeals to collectors that also sources grapes from Mendocino. Map B

Dutcher Crossing Winery – Dry Creek Valley – Charming and Relaxed – Wines: Zinfandel, Chardonnay, Cabernet Sauvignon, Merlot, Port, Petite Syrah, Sauvignon Blanc – 8533 Dry Creek Rd. Healdsburg CA 95448 – www.dutchercrossingwinery.com – (707) 431-2700 Hours: 11:00am–5:00pm – This is a small, family winery that is charming and popular. The tasting room is tiny and the winery is petite, but they produce some lovely wines often poured by the owners. Map F

Dutton Goldfield – Southwest Russian River Valley Tasting Room – Wines: Chardonnay, Pinot Noir, Syrah, Gewürztraminer, Zinfandel – 3100 Gravenstein Highway North, Sebastopol, CA 95472 – www.duttongoldfield.com – (707) 827-3600 – Hours 10:00am –4:30pm – The Dutton vineyards are highly respected for the quality of the wines they produce. Map E

Ektimo Vineyards – Southwest Russian River Valley – Wines: Chardonnay, Ektimo Brut, Zinfandel, Rose of Pinot Noir, Merlot – 4950 Ross Road Sebastopol, CA 95472 – www.ektimowines.com – (707) 827-3008 – Hours: Appointment – A surprisingly good winery in an older industrial building. Map E

Emeritus Vineyards – Southwest Russian River Valley – Wines: Bordeaux and Burgundy Blends – 2500 Gravenstein Highway N, Sebastopol, CA 95472 – www.emeritusvineyards.com– 707-823–9463 Hours: 10:30am to 4:00pm – They are in a modern building by the side of the road in a winery packed part of the valley. Map E

En Garde Winery – Sonoma Valley – Wines: Cabernet Sauvignon, Pinot Noir – Their location is changing, but expect that their tastings will be at a location along Sonoma Highway, Kenwood, CA 95452 – www.engardewinery.com – (707) 282-9216

Enkidu Wine – Sonoma Eighth Street Wineries Corporate Park Wines: Sauvignon Blanc, Syrah, Petite Syrah, Rhone Blends, Zinfandel, Pinot Noir, Cabernet Sauvignon – 21481 8th St. East Unit #1 Sonoma, CA 95476 – www.enkiduwines.com – (707) 939-3930 Hours: Appointment – They source fruit from Sonoma, Napa and Lake Counties. Map B

Eric Ross Winery – Glenn Ellen Tasting Room – Wines: Viognier, Chardonnay, Pinot Noir, Carignane, Zinfandel, Syrah, Zinfandel–Syrah Port, Marsanne–Rousanne, Port – 14300 Arnold Dr. Glen Ellen CA 95442 – www.ericross.com – (707) 939-8525 – Hours: 11:30–6:00pm Wednesday – Sunday. Map D

F. Teldeschi Winery – Dry Creek Valley – Four Generations – Wines: Zinfandel, Port, Pink Zinfandel, Petite Syrah – 3555 Dry Creek Rd. Healdsburg CA 95448 – www.teldeschi.com – (707) 433-6626 – Hours: 12:00pm–5:00pm – There is so much wonderful history related to both Italy and Dry Creek Valley here that the family story alone is enough to bring you through the door. Most of their extensive vineyards are planted to Zinfandel, including many old vines, although they have a wide variety of grapes on their land. They always believed in the potential of Zinfandel and boy were they right! Dry Creek Zinfandel is practically the standard against which all else is measured. For many years, they sold their grapes to other wineries, including the famous Zinfandel of Ravenswood. Then the next generation took the plunge and started their own winery. The two Teldeschi brothers, John and Dan, create the wine from vineyard to bottle. They are conveniently located at the intersection of Dry Creek Road and Lytton Springs Road. They claim to be one hundred paces from the Dry Creek General Store, but they must have long legs. But that is a great place to get lunch. The tasting room is bright and friendly. We would suggest that you visit here earlier in the day because the front of the tasting room is glass and faces west, so late in the day it gets pretty bright in there. Map F

Fathia Vineyards – Kenwood Tasting Room – Wines: Pinot Noir, Moscato, Cabernet Sauvignon, Sauvignon Blanc – 8910 Sonoma Highway, Kenwood, CA 95452 – www.fathiawines.com 707–363-4859– Hours: Appointment – info@fathiawines.com – Optional Pairing – Add a small plate of delightful cheeses to enhance your flight.

Ferrari-Carano Vineyards and Winery – Dry Creek Valley's Crown Jewel – Wines: Fumé Blanc, Zinfandel, Merlot, Malbec, Bordeaux blend, Grenache Rose, Dessert wines: Eldorado Gold (Semillon/Sauv blend) and Eldorado Noir (Black Muscat grape) – 8761 Dry Creek Rd. Healdsburg CA 95448 – www.ferrari–carano.com – (800) 831-0381 Hours: 10:00am – 5:00pm –

This is Dry Creek's largest winery. Don't miss the gardens hidden behind the wall to the right as you approach. Go downstairs to the Enoteca and see the barrel caves that stretch between the tasting room and the winery. The Japanese style winery was built first, and then later, the Italianate–style visitor's center. They have a separate winery for the reds and the whites. In the Enoteca, rather than pour their reserve wines, they offer wines that are made in small lots, often two and three hundred cases. It is a wonderful experience. The only problem is that it doesn't have the great views of the tasting room upstairs. Map F

Fisher Vineyards – In the hills between Santa Rosa and St. Helena, on top of a hill, and in Calistoga – Wines: Cabernet Sauvignon, Cabernet Franc, Syrah, Chardonnay – 6200 St Helena Road Santa Rosa, CA 95404 – (707) 539-7511 – Hours: Appointment – www.fishervineyards.com – This is a small, boutique winery. The original winery is up the narrow winding road that turns into Spring Mountain Road, leading down into Napa. The house sits at the top of a narrow driveway. They also have vineyards and a winery on their property in Northern Napa.

Flanagan Wines – Southern Dry Creek Valley – Wines: Chardonnay, Pinot Noir, Cabernet Sauvignon, Viognier, Merlot, Syrah – 435 W Dry Creek Road Healdsburg, CA 95448 – Hours: 10:00am to 5:00pm – Appointment – www.flanaganwines.com – This is a lovely winery at the south end of the Dry Creek Valley, close to the border of Russian River Valley. But their location does not reflect their wines since they have vineyards in Bennett Valley and the Petaluma Gap, among other places. They also purchase grapes from other producers. Map F

Flowers Winery – Russian River Valley – Wines: Pinot Noir, Chardonnay, Rosé – 4035 Westside Road Healdsburg, CA 95448 – www.flowerswinery.com – 707-723–4800 – Hours: Appointment – www.flowerswinery.com – reservations@flowerswinery.com – This is a long-time, highly respected producer of Pinot, going back to when the varietal was rarely planted.

In recent years it was purchased by Quintessa of Napa, who subsequently purchased this great property on Westside Road, south of Healdsburg, which they renovated and expanded, before moving Flowers there. It is an elegant tasting now, and in demand so make your appointments early. At the time when Flowers first became well known they stood far above the small number of other Pinot producers, a very finicky grape. But today, there are numerous premium and ultra-premium wineries in the area at that level. Still, it is well worth the visit. Map E

Fog Crest Vineyard – Southern Russian River – Wines: Pinot Noir, Chardonnay, Rosé – 7606 Occidental Road Sebastopol, CA 95472 www.fogcrestvineyard.com – (707) 829-2006 – Hours: 11:00am–5:00pm – Appointment – www.fogcrestvineyard.com – This is a small, charming family winery that is perched on the top of a hill with great views. Map E

Foley Sonoma Winery – Mid-Alexander Valley – Wines: Cabernet Sauvignon, Merlot, Syrah, Zinfandel, Pinot Noir, Blends, Chardonnay, Rosé – 5110 Highway 128 Geyserville CA 95448 – www.foleysonoma.com – (707) 433-1944 opt 1 – Hours: 11:00–5:00pm – They are located in a very modern building with great views and wonderful picnic areas. This award-winning building would be enough of a reason to come here, but the great views, the lovely picnic tables, good wines, and nice staff offer sufficient reason to visit by themselves. The views of the valley to the north look over the old vines that produce some of their wines. From their tasting room you can look through the panoramic windows, stroll out onto the patios, or peer down into their cavernous barrel cellar where they often host events at banquet tables. As you arrive, there is a spacious lawn with tables for picnics, with restrooms just to the right. As you walk past that, if you look over the railing, below you will see an outdoor wedding chapel by a fountain. They are just around the corner from the Robert Young Winery, the Hawkes Winery, and Stonestreet. Map G

Foppiano Vineyards – Just south of Downtown Healdsburg known for their Petite Sirah – Wines: Zinfandel, Merlot, Chardonnay, Sangiovese, Cabernet Sauvignon, Pinot Noir, Petite Sirah, White Zinfandel – 12707 Old Redwood Highway Healdsburg CA 95448 – www.foppiano.com – (707) 433-7272 Hours: 10:00am to 4:30pm – Self guided tour – This is one of the older wineries from this area that still consistently produces a good product. While the outside looks like farm buildings, they have a charming tasting room with a nice staff, pretty views of the vineyards and a nice gift selection. Next to the tasting room is a cute caboose. Map E

Fort Ross Vineyard, Winery – On the Sonoma Coast North of the Russian River – Wines: Chardonnay, Pinot Noir – 15725 Meyers Grade Road Jenner, CA 95450 – (707) 847-3460 – www.fortrossvineyard.com – Hours: Appointment – This beautiful winery sits on the hills overlooking the Pacific Ocean a short distance north of where the Russian River empties in the ocean, and a little south of the historic Fort Ross, Russia's last outpost in California. Winery wise, they have this area to themselves, so to deal with the fact that visitors have made them the destination, they offer wonderful food pairings to go with their wines. That bright sun and cool ocean breezes produce vineyards in this area that produce some of America's best Pinot Noir and Chardonnay. But, the area also comes with its hazards that make grape growing here challenging, birds, winds and fog.

Kosta Browne Winery – Sebastopol at the Barlow Center – 200 Morris St, Sebastopol, CA 95472 – (707) 823-7430 – www.kostabrowne.com – Hours: Appointment for Wine Club Members This is a popular wine for collectors available through their wine club, and typically they have a waiting list. Their winery is located at the rear of the popular Barlow center in downtown Sebastopol, which is a great collection of restaurants, shops, galleries and tasting rooms. If you are touring in the southern part of the Russian River Valley including a visit to the Barlow center will give you some great insights about the local culture.

Francis Ford Coppola Winery – Alexander Valley – Family Friendly – Wines: Chardonnay, Pinot Noir, Syrah, Viognier, Cabernet Sauvignon, Zinfandel, Claret, Merlot, Malbec, Syrah–Shiraz, Pinot Grigio, Blanc de Blanc Sparkling wine, Rosé – 300 Via Archimedes Geyserville CA 95448 – www.franciscoppolawinery.com – (707) 857-1400 – Hours: 10:00am–5:00pm – This expansive property went through several owners including Coppola, who placed his medium range labels here, separating it from his Inglenook label in Napa. He since sold FFC to the family owned Delicato winery. It is a destination suitable for families to visit with a restaurant that expands onto large patios which is surrounded by some of its vineyards. There is a pool with cabanas and another bar style restaurant there. There are tasting bars downstairs and upstairs. The most exceptional attraction is the large collection of movie props from the director's career which are found throughout. In the busy season if you want to eat at the restaurant make reservations. Map G

Francis Ford Coppola Too – Alexander Valley – Previously Called Virginia Dare Winery – Wines: Appointment – 22281 Chianti Rd. Geyserville CA 95441 – www.ffcwtoo.com – (707) 735-3500 – Hours: 11:00am–5:00pm Friday–Sunday – Appointment – This is a smaller facility that Delicato bought in July of 2021, so expect changes. Map G

Freestone Vineyards – May be Closed to Visitors – Far Southwestern Russian River – Wines: Pinot Noir, Chardonnay – 12747 El Camino Bodega, Freestone CA 95448 – www.jpvfreestone.com – (707) 874-1010 – This winery has been closed to visitors for long periods of time, so check to see if they are open for tastings – Hours: 11:00am–5:00pm Friday, Saturday and Sunday – This winery, owned by the Joseph Phelps Vineyards, is on the road to Bodega Bay. They chose this site for its ability to grow great Burgundy style wines, something which the Phelps' up valley location in Napa can't do. On the other hand, this winery is not close to many others, so from time to time they close the tasting room. So check to see if they are open to the public. If you are interested in tasting these great wines they also pour them at the Joseph Phelps Winery in the Napa Valley, along with the rest of their wines. They are located quite close to the Ocean on the beautiful Sonoma Coast. Map E

Frick Winery – Edge of Dry Creek Valley and Alexander Valley – Tucked Away – Wines: Syrah, Viognier, Cinsault, Grenache, Counoise, Grenache Blanc and Merlot – 23072 Walling Rd. Geyserville CA 95441 – www.frickwinery.com – (707) 857-1980 – Hours: 12–4:30 Saturday and Sunday – This is a small winery tucked away in the eastern hillsides of the Dry Creek Valley. They have limited hours, but the wines are hand made by the owner, and they focus on the Rhone varietals, which are not common in this area, so they are a nice change of pace. The tasting is in a charming, little cottage, that cannot handle a lot of people, and the parking lot is only suitable for about five cars. The views are beautiful although the buildings are in charming disrepair, or at least they were the most recent time we were there so check them out and let us know. Map F

Fritz Underground Winery – Tasting in the Cave at the northern Edge of Dry Creek Valley – Wines: Chardonnay, Pinot Noir, Zinfandel, Cabernet Sauvignon, Sauvignon Blanc – 24691 Dutcher Creek Rd. Cloverdale CA 95425 – www.fritzwinery.com – (707) 894-3389 – Hours: 10:30am–4:30pm – The winery was started in 1979 and they reduced their quantity in favor of quality sourcing grapes from Russian River and Dry Creek. The gravity winery is entirely inside the cave. The wines are nicely priced and the chance to visit a hillside cave winery is not that common in this part of Sonoma. This is very much a family run operation that is looking to the future. They are fairly far north in the valley, but worth the ride. Map F

Furthermore Winery – Southern Russian River Valley – Wines: Chardonnay, Pinot Noir – 3541 Gravenstein Highway N, Sebastopol, CA 95472 – www.furthermorewines.com –
(707) 823-3040 – Hours: 10:00am to 4:30pm – Map E

Garden Creek Ranch and Vineyard – Alexander Valley – Wines: Bordeaux and Burgundy – 2335 Geysers Rd, Geyserville, CA 95441 – www.gardencreekvineyards.com – (707) 433-8345 – Hours: Appointment – This is a small family winery run by a couple who grew up in the area. It is a totally authentic, charming experience and the wines are wonderful. Map G

Gary Farrell Vineyards and Winery – Russian River Valley Just North of the River – Spectacular Location – Wines: Chardonnay, Pinot Noir, Zinfandel, Merlot, Cabernet Sauvignon, Blends – 10701 Westside Rd. Healdsburg CA 95448 – www.garyfarrellwines.com – (707) 473-2900 – Hours: 11:00am–4:00pm
The winery is up a long, steep driveway on a hill overlooking the Russian River Valley below. The tasting room is in a modern building that enjoys wonderful views to the south. They are ten minutes off River Road, over some winding roads, but it is a pretty ride, and it is a place that you will remember. Navigation: Reach them from River Road onto Wohler Road. Look for the pole with all the winery signs on it. At the Y in the road, by the Bed and Breakfast on the hill, bear left. Follow that over the one lane bridge, and then at the intersection of Westside Road turn left. The very steep winery drive will be on the right side. Map F

Glenlyon Vineyards and Winery – Sonoma Valley to Bennett Valley – Wines: Rose, Syrah, Rouge – 2750 John Hill Road Glen Ellen, CA 95442 – www.glenlyonwinery.com – (707) 484-0077 Hours: Appointment – Squire@GlenLyonWinery.com – This is a charming family winery moving into its second generation on the hills of the Bennett Valley to the west of Glen Ellen. They are well-known for their Syrah but all the wines are good. The winery tour and tasting with the owner is exceptional, but plan to buy when you visit because the wines are that good. Map D

Gloria Ferrer Caves and Vineyards – Los Carneros – Sparkling Wines and Great Location – Wines: Sparkling, Blanc de Blancs, Brut, Blanc de Noirs, Cuvee, Brut Rosé, Chardonnay, Pinot Noir, Syrah – 23555 Carneros Highway. 121 Sonoma

CA 95476 – www.gloriaferrer.com – (707) 996-7256 – Hours: 10:00am–5:00pm – They produce good, well–priced sparklers and their tasting room patio is a great place to enjoy them. They are more of a bar than a tasting room, but with the views and location who cares. Being in Los Carneros, they make a great first or last stop on a trip up from the city. They are owned by a large Spanish winery so they don't have a family winery feel, however, they've been in Sonoma long enough to absorb that wonderful hospitality that is famous here. Map B

Gopfrich – Dry Creek Valley – Wines: Cabernet Sauvignon, Zinfandel, Syrah – 7462 W. Dry Creek Rd. Healdsburg CA 95448 – www.gopfrich.com – (707) 433-1645 – Hours: Appointment – This is a small production, family run estate located in the north western part of the Dry Creek Valley. The wines are only available there and the tastings are by appointment. Map F

Gordenker – Sonoma Valley – Wines: Sauvignon Blanc, Pinot Noir, Cabernet Sauvignon, Rose – Tasting Room – 12201 CA–12, Glen Ellen, CA 95442 – (707) 934-7759 – Hours: Appointment – michele@gordenker.com – This is a small family vineyard started in 1946.

Graton Ridge Winery – Russian River Valley – Charming Small Tasting Room – Wines: Sauvignon Blanc, Chardonnay, Rose, Zinfandel, Pinot Noir, Cabernet Sauvignon, Zinfandel Port, Apple Port – 3561 Gravenstein Highway N. Sebastopol, CA 95472 – www.gratonridge.com – (707) 823-3040 – Hours: 10:00am–4:30pm Friday–Monday – This is a cute little place with a great staff and lovely wines that sits amid the apple groves along the Gravenstein Highway. From the outside, it seems low key, but inside it is a charming experience with a comfortable bar, and some pretty features, murals and lovely gift items. Map E

Gundlach Bundschu Winery – Sonoma Valley – The Rhinefarm – Wines: Zinfandel, Gewürztraminer, Chardonnay, Pinot Noir, Cabernet Franc, Merlot, Cabernet Sauvignon – 2000 Denmark

St. Sonoma CA 95448 – www.gunbun.com – (707) 938-3015 – Hours: 11:00am–4:00pm – Located minutes from the Sonoma Plaza and started as a farm in 1858, it is still in the same family. This is the southern edge of the Sonoma Valley, near Los Carneros so these are good food wines, typical of that cool climate. They have a nice picnic patio with a pretty view, and a short cave tour. There are hiking trails nearby but watch out for the rattlesnakes. Map B

Gustafson Family Vineyard – Northern Tip of Dry Creek Valley 9100 Skaggs Springs Road, Geyserville – www.gfvineyard.com – (707) 433-2371 – Hours: 10:00am to 6:00pm – Appointment – Picnic Area – This family vineyard and winery is at the northern edge of the Dry Creek Valley, just south of Lake Sonoma and past Ferrari Carano and Sbragia family. So you need to be heading there, because there are no other wineries nearby, but it is a great place to grow grapes. Map F

Hamel Family Wines – Sonoma Valley – Wines: Zinfandel, Sauvignon Blanc, Rose – 15401 Sonoma Highway, Sonoma, CA 95476 (707)–996-5800 – Hours: 10:00am to 5:00pm Appointment – www.hamelfamilywines.com – This is a beautiful, biodynamic winery a short ride north of the Sonoma Plaza. The tasting includes a tour of the winery. The hospitality building is modern and elegant with great views. These slopes had been farmed for a long time by one of the local Italian American families before the Hamel family purchased it. Map D

Hanna Winery – Alexander Valley with Great Views – Wines: Merlot, Zinfandel, Pinot Noir, Cabernet Sauvignon, Sauvignon Blanc, Syrah, Blends, Cabernet Franc, Rosé – 9280 Highway 128 Healdsburg CA 95448 – www.hannawinery.com – (707) 575-3371 – Hours: 10:00am–5:00pm – This winery is located at the lower edge of the Alexander Valley in a spectacular location with great views of the valley and the distant hills. They make big reds with lots of depth and softness. They have a charming building with a pleasant staff. When you are coming to Alexander Valley from Napa (Calistoga) via Knight's Valley on Route 128, this makes a nice first stop. Map G

Hanna Winery – Russian River Valley – Wines: Merlot, Zinfandel, Pinot Noir, Cabernet Sauvignon, Sauvignon Blanc, Syrah, Blends, Cabernet Franc, Rosé – 5353 Occidental Rd Santa Rosa CA 95401 – www.hannawinery.com – (707) 575-3371 – Hours: 10:00am–4:00pm – These are the Russian River vineyards and tasting room connected with the Alexander Valley winery. It is a charming tasting room and the wines are good. They are near Balleto, Dutton Goldfield, Lynmar and Graton Ridge. Map E

Hanzell Vineyards – Sonoma Valley – Historic Pinot Noir – Wines: Chardonnay, Pinot Noir – 18596 Lomita Ave. Sonoma CA 95476 – www.hanzell.com – (707) 996-3860 – Hours: Appointment – These are among California's oldest Pinot Noir and Chardonnay vineyards, which are planted on hillsides, and can be seen from downtown Sonoma. They include a significant portion of the original vines, so the production is small, about one ton per acre, although some replanting has been done recently. They do their tastings by appointment, but allow extra time to get there because they are reached via a winding, climbing gravel road, but they are worth the effort. They do a vineyard, cave and winery tour and a sit–down tasting in a great old building patterned on a classic French winemaking building. They also do a true reserve selection from their extensive collection. The tastings are expensive by Sonoma standards, but for the serious aficionado it is worth the price. The tour and tasting is not rushed so plan on spending a couple of hours there. They have spectacular views of Sonoma and the southern valley. Map D

Hartford Family Winery – Russian River Valley – Lovely Wines from Green Valley – Wines: Pinot Noir, Chardonnay, Zinfandel – 8075 Martinelli Rd. Forestville CA 95436 – www.hartfordwines.com – (707) 887-8010 – Hours: 10:00am–4:30pm – They are located on a side road that stretches between River Road and Gravenstein Highway. They make some nice wines in a pretty location. The building has some of the classic, French style architecture that you see at Kendall Jackson. Map E

Harvest Moon Estate – Russian River Valley – A Little Jewel of a Winery – Wines: Zinfandel, Gewürztraminer, Sparkling Gewürztraminer, Pinot Noir – 2192 Olivet Rd. Santa Rosa CA 95401 – www.harvestmoonwinery.com – (707) 573-8711 – Hours: 10:30am–5:00pm – This is a charming, small winery, with a pretty building, that makes lovely wines. It is one of the Olivet Road wineries, so the vineyards produce dependable and enjoyable flavors. The tasting is low–key and friendly, and they do great events. Map E

Hawkes Wines – Alexander Valley Tasting Room – Wines: Chardonnay, Merlot, Cabernet Sauvignon – 6734 Highway 128 Healdsburg CA 95448 – www.hawkeswine.com – (707) 433-4295 – Hours: 10:00am–5:00pm The Hawkes family has been growing grapes for quite a while in Alexander Valley and they have some wonderful vineyards up on the hillsides to the east of their tasting room. Great grapes make great wines. The staff is gracious and quite knowledgeable, and the tasting room is roomy and nicely appointed. Map G

Hawley Wines – Downtown Healdsburg Tasting Room – Wines: Wide Variety – 36 North St Healdsburg CA 95448 – www.hawleywine.com – (707) 473-9500 – Hours: 11:00am–6:00pm – This tasting room is just steps from the Healdsburg plaza. They make fine, moderately priced wines, and they have a good staff. Their wines come from their own organic hillside vineyards overlooking the Dry Creek Valley. They make a wide variety.

Holdredge Wines – Downtown Healdsburg – Wines: Pinot Noir – 51 Front St. Healdsburg CA 95448 – www.holdredge.com – (707) 431-1424 – Hours: 11:00am–4:30pm Saturday – Sunday – This is a small winery that handcrafts their Russian River Pinot Noir. They have limited tasting room hours and only make about 3,000 cases. However, they are conveniently located nearby other tasting rooms, so when you go touring in Healdsburg on the weekend, check them out.

Homewood Winery – Los Carneros – Authentic Handmade – Wines: Sauvignon Blanc, Chardonnay, Pinot Noir, Grenache, Merlot, Syrah, Zinfandel, Blends – 23120 Burndale Rd. Vineburg CA 95487 – www.homewoodwinery.com – (707) 996-6353 – Hours: 10:00am–4:00pm – This is a completely authentic Sonoma winery, with the tanks just on the other side of the wall from the tasting bar. The winemaker and owner is David Homewood and he is often on hand to chat about the wines, which are good. In the warmer weather, the tastings are done outside on the picnic tables. Although the winery is located in the Los Carneros district, David buys his grapes from various sources, including Napa so he can pick and choose the best. They are located just off Highways 121/12. Map B

Hook and Ladder Winery – Russian River – Olivet Rd – Wines: Cabernet Sauvignon, Zinfandel, White Zinfandel, Pinot Noir, Chardonnay, Gewürztraminer, Rosé – 2134 Olivet Rd. Santa Rosa CA 95401 – www.hookandladderwinery.com – (707) 526-2255 – Hours: 10:00am–4:30pm – This is a small winery that makes some wonderful wines and offers them in a casual setting with the tanks and barrels in site of the tasting bar. The walls are decorated with Firehouse emblems and if you show your card as a volunteer or full-time fireman tastings are free. Olivet Road has a number of gems. Map E

Hop Kiln Winery – Russian River Valley – Architectural Destination – Wines: Cabernet Sauvignon, Chardonnay, Riesling, Zinfandel – 6050 Westside Rd. Healdsburg CA 95448 – www.hopkilnwinery.com – (707) 433-6491 – Hours: 10:00am–5:00pm – They are located halfway up Westside Road in a beautifully restored Hop Kiln from years past when this was an important hop growing area. There are pictures along the walls showing the fascinating history of the place. They have a great gift area including lots of foods, snacks and chocolate. They make good value wines including some unusual blends, poured by a friendly staff. This is a nice place for a picnic and a great place to stop later in the day when some of your party might be more interested in shopping than tasting. They are owned by Landmark Vineyards and are referred to as Landmark at Hop Kiln. Map E

Idell Family Vineyards – Sonoma Valley – Wines: Chardonnay, Syrah Zinfandel – 18900 Carriger Road Sonoma CA – (707) 938-7765 – Appointment – www.idellfamilyvineyards.com – An interesting family winery west of downtown Sonoma. Map B

Imagery Estate Winery – Sonoma Valley – Art Lover Destination – Wines: Cabernet Franc, Petite Syrah, Barbera, Sangiovese, Malbec, White Burgundy, Pinot Blanc, Viognier, Port – 14335 Highway 12 Glen Ellen CA 95442 – www.imagerywinery.com – (877) 550-4278 – Hours: 10:00am–5:00pm – This place is a jewel, pouring small lot wines that include many unusual varietals only sold at the winery. After commissioning art for labels for many years, they created the world's largest collection of art created expressly for labels, which was donated to Sonoma State University by the family. But the new owners have continued the label tradition and those painting are displayed in the tasting room. The staff will share the story with you, and the book cataloging the collection is often on the bar. This is connected to the Benziger Family Winery and they will often give you a coupon for a tasting there. They have picnic tables, bocce courts, a nice gift area with unique items related to their labels, and extensive picnic areas. Navigation: They share a driveway with the Arrowood Winery. As you come north from the Sonoma Plaza, after you pass the B.R. Cohn winery on the left–hand side, their driveway will come up on the right side just past the curve. Look for the banners. Map D

Inman Family – Russian River Valley Olivet Road – Wines: Rose, Pinot Noir, Sparkling, Chardonnay – 3900 Piner Road Santa Rosa, CA 95401 – www.inmanfamilywines.com – (707)

293–9576 – Hours: 11:00am–5:00pm – Appointment – this is a lovely little winery with wonderful wines made in small lots by the owner, Kathleen Inman. Map E

Iron Horse Vineyards – Russian River Valley – Great Views – Wines: Chardonnay, Pinot Noir, Viognier, Sangiovese, Merlot, Cabernet Sauvignon, Multiple Sparkling Wines – 9786 Ross Station Rd. Sebastopol CA 95472 – www.ironhorsevineyards.com – (707) 887-1507 Hours: 11:00am–3:30pm – This is a pet friendly, beautiful location, situated down a narrow road. The tasting is outside under a lean–to, looking east out over the hills. The staff is friendly, the wines are great, and the experience is not to be missed. Get there early in the day when you can enjoy the morning sunshine, they open at 11 and they close early. Their wines tend to be lighter and it makes them a good first stop in the Russian River Valley. They are in wide distribution, but there you will taste their small production wines that are only available at the winery. Map E

J Vineyards and Winery – Russian River Valley – Sparkling Wines and Great Pairings – Wines: Pinot Noir, Pinot Gris, Chardonnay, Vin Gris, Pear Liqueur, Rosé – 11447 Old Redwood Highway. Healdsburg CA 95448 – www.jwine.com – (707) 431-5430 – Hours: 11:00am–5:00pm – This is a wonderful sparkling and still wine producer that does great food pairings in an elegant setting. They share a driveway with Rodney Strong. They have a nice gift section and a friendly staff. This is a great place to end a day of tasting, which may explain why they get so busy late in the day. The place is a lot of fun. The food pairings are well known, and while you can sometimes arrange them on a walk in basis, it is better to set up an appointment. Map E

J. Rickards Winery – Alexander Valley – Wines: Sauvignon Blanc, Rose, Zinfandel, Syrah, Cabernet Sauvignon – 24505 Chianti Road Cloverdale, CA 95425 – www.jrwinery.com – (707) 758-3441 – Hours: 11:00am–5:00pm Monday – Saturday – info@jrwinery.com. Map G

J. Rochioli Vineyards and Winery – Russian River Valley – A White House Wine – Wines: Sauvignon Blanc, Chardonnay, Pinot Noir – 6192 Westside Rd. Healdsburg CA 95448 www.rochioliwinery.com (707) 433-2305 – Hours: 11:00am–4:00pm – This is a small tasting room hidden away in the Russian River Valley. They can be tricky to spot sometimes, but they are located just south of the hard to miss Hop Kiln Winery, on the same side of the road. They produce great wines, but most of it goes to their wine club, so when you visit, the list they pour from may be small. Their wines have been poured at the White House for many years. This is a pretty place with great views of the vineyards along the river. Map E

Jacuzzi Family Vineyards – Los Carneros – Wines: Chardonnay, Pinot Noir, Barbera, Sangiovese, Arneis, Merlot, Nebbiolo, Primitivo, Pinot Grigio, Moscato Blanc – 24724 Arnold Dr. Sonoma CA 95476 – www.jacuzziwines.com – (707) 931-7575 – Hours: 10:00am–5:00pm – This is an Italian style winery owned by Cline, located across the street. They have a big spacious tasting room, specializing in Italian varietals. The Olive Press shares the building so you can also do an olive oil tasting. Both sides of the building have gift shops. This is a wonderful place to visit because there is something for everyone, both the wine lover and the shopper. It is convenient to San Francisco via the Golden Gate Bridge. They make a great first or last stop on a tour originating in the city. The wines are very good, refreshing and well made. It has wonderful Italian style architecture, gardens and expansive event spaces. Map B

Jigar Wines – Forestville Tasting Room – Wines: Cabernet Sauvignon, Pinot Noir, Merlot, Chardonnay, Syrah – 6615 Front St, Forestville, CA 95436 – www.jigarwines.com – (707) 820-1225 – Hours: 11:00am–5:00pm.

Jordan Vineyard and Winery – Alexander Valley – Famous Reds Wines: Cabernet Sauvignon, Chardonnay, Dessert Wine, Olive Oil – 1474 Alexander Valley Rd. Healdsburg CA 95448

www.jordanwinery.com – (707) 431-5250 – Hours: Appointment Tours Monday – Saturday Closed Sunday – This is a grand estate in the Alexander Valley, with a wonderful staff and well regarded Bordeaux–style wines. This tasting is for the serious wine lover, since the wines are expensive. They are by appointment with limited slots so plan well in advance. They do both tastings and tours at different times. The sign on Alexander Valley Road is small, but the driveway entrance is quite broad and well done. If you are coming from Healdsburg, it is on the right side. It looks like a French Chateau by intention. The big difference is that the Alexander Valley has nicer weather than Bordeaux. Map G

Joseph Jewell – Forestville Tasting Room – Wines: Pinot Noir, Chardonnay – 6542 Front St, Forestville, CA 95436 – www.josephjewell.com – (707) 820-1621 – Hours: 11:00am to 7:00pm Thursday – Monday, Closed Tuesday and Wednesday – info@josephjewell.com.

Joseph Swan Vineyards – Russian River Valley – Rustic and Charming – Wines: Zinfandel, Pinot Noir, Syrah – 2916 Laguna Rd. Forestville CA 95436 – www.swanwinery.com – (707) 573-3747 – Hours: 11:00am–4:00pm Appointment. This long time, small, family winery is just off River Road with wonderful views of the vineyards. You walk past the bins and tanks to get to the tasting room, which doubles as the barrel room. They also taste outsidde on the patio. The whole experience is country and friendly and well worth the ride. The wines are good. Limited to groups of 8 or less. Map E

Keller Estate – Petaluma Over the Western Hills from Los Carneros A Unique Estate – Wines: Rosé, Chardonnay, Pinot Gris, Pinot Noir, Syrah – 5875 Lakeville Highway. Petaluma CA 95954 – www.kellerestate.com – (707) 765-2117 – Hours: 11:00am–4:00pm. Thursday – Sunday – This is an expansive vineyard and winery located off Highway 101 in Petaluma, which makes it convenient to San Francisco. The winemaking facility and the grounds and buildings are grand. They have a good tour and a nice art collection spread around the grounds. They are a bit off the beaten tour track but worth the effort. There is a race car track that runs through the property because the owners are big fans of the sport.

Kendall-Jackson – Russian River Valley – A Famous Brand – Wines: Cabernet Sauvignon, Merlot, Syrah, Chardonnay, Pinot Noir, Riesling, Sauvignon Blanc, Zinfandel, Olive Oil – 5007 Fulton Rd. Fulton CA 95439 – www.kj.com – (707) 433-7102 – Hours: 10:00am – 5:00pm – This is essentially a very big tasting room surrounded by vineyards, including a wonderful demonstration vineyard. You can see the French style building from Highway 101. Map E

Kenwood Vineyards Winery – Sonoma Valley – Wines: Cabernet Sauvignon, Chardonnay, Sauvignon Blanc, Zinfandel, Pinot Noir, Merlot, Gewürztraminer – 9592 Sonoma Highway. Kenwood CA 95452 – www.kenwoodvineyards.com – (707) 833-5891 – Hours: 10:00am–4:30pm – They are located in the center of Kenwood Because the winery sits on a slight rise, it provides a pleasant view of the vines and the town of Kenwood. Their Jack London Vineyards from Sonoma Mountain wines stand out. Yes, the famous writer of Call of the Wild lived just up the road. Map D

Kivelstadt Cellars – Downtown Sonoma –Wines: Syrah, Sauvignon Blanc, Zinfandel , Pinot Noir – 22900 Broadway Sonoma, CA 95476 – www.kivelstadtcellars.com – (707) 938-7001 – Hours: 12:00pm to 5:00pm.

Kobler Estate Winery – Russian River Valley – Wines: Sauvignon Blanc, Syrah, Rose , Chardonnay, Pinot Noir – 4630 Gravenstein Highway North, Sebastopol, California 95472 – www.koblerestatewinery.com – (707) 473-8287 – 11:00am–5:00pm – Appointment – info@koblerestatewinery.com. Very small family winery with four acres plus of vineyards. Map E

Kokomo Wines – Dry Creek Valley at the Timber Crest Center – Wines: Sauvignon Blanc, Chardonnay, Pinot Noir, Zinfandel, Cabernet Sauvignon, Syrah, Petite Syrah – 4791 Dry Creek Road Healdsburg CA 95448 – www.kokomowines.com – (707) 433-0200 – Hours: 11:00am–4:30pm – This is a newer winery based on long term vineyards located just behind the property. The tasting room is also the winery, and the sense of being right where everything happens is fun. They make good wines and have a basic tasting room. Being located in the Timber Crest Center, they are walking distance to other good wineries so it creates a nice social scene, especially later in the day. Map F

Korbel Champagne Cellars – Russian River Valley – Historic Location – Wines: Sparkling and Still wines – 13250 River Rd. Guerneville CA 95446 – www.korbel.com – (707) 824-7000 – Hours: 10:00am–5:00pm (4:30 in Winter) – This is one of California's oldest sparkling wine houses, founded in 1882 by two Polish brothers. They are located on River Road, on the way to the Pacific Ocean, just outside of downtown Guerneville. The fog and cool air that flows in from the sea help to create conditions that suit Chardonnay and Pinot Noir perfectly. The tasting room is spacious with a nice gift area. Korbel's market is one of the best local places to stop for lunch with lots of seating outdoors among the redwood trees. Most people know the Korbel label as a modestly priced, sparkling wine, but when you visit here, you will taste and buy wines that are only sold at the winery. Between the lovely valley breezes, the history, frequent tours, architecture and deli, what's not to like? Map E

Kunde Family Estate - Sonoma Valley – Five Generations Wines: Sauvignon Blanc, Chardonnay, Syrah, Zinfandel, Merlot, Cabernet Sauvignon, Primitivo, Sangiovese, Barbera, Gewürztraminer, Grenache Rosé, Meritage, Zinfandel Port – 9825 Sonoma Highway, Kenwood CA 95452 – www.kunde.com – (707) 833-5501 – Hours: 10:30–4:30 – The Kunde family farms their land in one of the most beautiful parts of the Valley of the Moon. Across the road is a charming restaurant in case you need a place for lunch. Besides a friendly tasting bar, Kunde offers a wonderful sit–down reserve tasting. They also do guided tours of their barrel caves, behind the winery under the beautifully terraced, vine covered hillsides. They also do tastings on top of the hill under the trees with views of the valley. For many years they sold a wide variety of grapes to other wineries, and then, in the early 1990's, they started making their own wine. As a result, they offer a wonderful variety and the wines are a great deal for the quality. The tasting room and winery building is based on a Georgian style cow barn that sat on the site for many years. They have picnic tables outside by the fountain, nice gifts, and a wonderful ambience. They are a great value and the place is a lot of fun. Bring a picnic and enjoy the view and the wines. Groups of 10 or more should call ahead. Map D

La Crema Estate at Saralee's Vineyard – Russian River Valley – Wines: Pinot Noir, Pinot Gris, Pinot Rose, Chardonnay, Syrah, Viognier – 3575 Slusser Rd. Windsor, CA 95492 – www.lacrema.com – (707) 431-9400 – Hours: 10:00am –5:30pm – This is a large winery for a well-known brand, located near the Sonoma Airport on the north side of River Road. The tasting is in an historic barn built in 1900. Map E

La Follette Wines – Transitioning – Wines: Pinot Noir – They are currently offering tastings at the Quivera Winery – www.lafollettewines.com – 707–431-8333 – Hours: 11:00am–5:00pm.

Lago di Merlo Vineyard and Winery – Dry Creek Valley – Wines: Lago di Merlo, Chardonnay, Sangiovese, Rosato, Amanti II – 3495 Skagg's Spring Rd. Geyserville CA 95441 – www.lagodimerlo.com – (707)473-0146 – Hours: Appointment – They are located at the very top of Dry Creek Valley just south of Lake Sonoma so make an appointment before you go. Map F

Lambert Bridge Winery – A Dry Creek Jewel – Wines: Sauvignon Blanc, Chardonnay, Viognier, Zinfandel, Crane Creek Cuvée, Petite Syrah, Merlot, Cabernet Franc, Cabernet Sauvignon, oils and condiments – 4085 W. Dry Creek Rd. Healdsburg CA 95448 – www.lambertbridge.com – (707) 431-9600 – Hours: 10:30am–4:30pm Appointment – This is a beautiful, small winery, with a great picnic area, a nice gift collection, a knowledgeable and friendly staff, a great tasting room and spectacular wines. They run numerous events on their picnic grounds complete with an outdoor kitchen. They have both a basic and reserve tasting, and the best way to get their wines is through the wine club because their production is limited and the wines are popular. Many of their wines are distributed solely to their wine club. This area normally grows great grapes, so the variable becomes how much effort and labor the owners are willing to put into the farm work and winemaking. In Lambert Bridge's case, that means having three winemakers, state of the art equipment and a lot of money spent on new French oak barrels. This results in wines that compete well with Napa at Sonoma prices. Their seated pairing in the barrel room are very cool. Map F

Lancaster Estate Winery – Russian River Valley – At the southern edge of the Alexander Valley – An Ultra Premium Producer – Wines: Cabernet Sauvignon Blends, Sauvignon Blanc – 15001 Chalk Hill Rd. Healdsburg CA 95448 – www.lancaster–estate.com – (707) 433-8178 Hours: Tuesday – Saturday Appointment – This is a stunning, by appointment, smaller winery. The tastings are private and are conducted in the library room in their beautiful caves. They are located close to both the Chalk Hill and Knights Valley districts. Be serious when you make your appointment because there is a cancellation fee. This winery is for the enthusiast who likes big red wines in the Bordeaux style and who likes an exclusive experience. The staff is friendly and knowledgeable. The vineyards and winery are tucked into a lovely little valley. The fifty plus acres are planted to the classic Bordeaux red varietals. Even though they are technically in the Russian River Valley, they are more easily reached from Alexander Valley Road. While you can take Chalk Hill Road north to get there, past the Chalk Hill and Roth wineries, we don't recommend it because it is a narrow and winding road. Map E

Landmark Winery – Sonoma Valley – Wonderful Gardens – Wines: Chardonnay, Pinot Noir, Syrah and expanding each year in the Rhone Varietals – 101 Adobe Canyon Rd. Kenwood CA 95452 – www.landmarkwine.com (707) 833-0218 – Hours: 10:00am–4:30pm Appointment – This is lovely winery specializing in Burgundy and Rhone wines, The winery is built like a classic Spanish compound, with the buildings protecting an inner garden which is perfect for picnics and bocce. These are some of the prettiest and most comfortable winery grounds in wine country. The wines are excellent and have been served many times at the White House. A hidden treasure is the President's Tower tasting room where a private, seated tasting for eight can be scheduled. The walls are lined with White House menus from the past twenty years. The views from the tower tasting room take your breath away, including the expanse of the Valley of the Moon with Sugar Loaf Mountain and Hood Mountain in the distance. For such a low key, gracious winery, they produce a wonderful winery experience and of course, wonderful wines. You can see the winery from Highway 12, but you need to turn right on Adobe Canyon Road to reach the entrance. They are just north Chateau St. Jean. Map D

La Rochelle – Sonoma Valley – Wines: Pinot Noir, Chardonnay – 233 Adobe Canyon Road, Kenwood, CA 95452 – www.lrwine.com – (707) 302-8000 – Hours: 11:00am–5:00pm – Appointment – This is a charming family winery that produces wonderful Pinot Noir, as well as Chardonnay. It is very small and calling ahead for an appointment is a very good idea. They are located just past Landmark. Map D

Larson Family Winery – Los Carneros – Family Style – Wines: White and Red table wines, Chardonnay, Semi sweet Gewürztraminer, Cuveé Rosé, Pinot Noir Rosé, Pinot Noir, Merlot, Meritage, Petite Syrah, Cabernet Sauvignon, Pinot Grigio – 23355 Millerick Rd. Sonoma CA 95476 – www.LarsonFamilyWinery.com – (707) 938-3031 – Hours: 10:00am–5:00pm – This is as much a ranch as a winery and in all ways, a lot of fun for a family with kids. They have bocce, horses, and have a petting zoo with a picnic area and plenty of space for the kids to run around. This was the site of the Sonoma Rodeo and the pictures about its history are cool. The tasting room feels like a barn's tack room. Being a ranch, it is not as slick and polished as many of their neighboring wineries but well worth the visit. Map B

Lasseter Family Winery – Sonoma Valley – Beautiful seated tasting – Wines: A wide variety – 1 Vintage Lane Glen Ellen CA 95442 –www.lasseterfamilywinery.com – (707) 933-2800 – Hours: by Appointment – The winery of John and Nancy Lassiter. John is the head of Pixar and continues Sonoma's tradition of being a home to artists and animators. It is a pretty winery and a gracious tasting room. The art and style of the place is delightful. They do limited appointments, but they are easy to arrange and it is near Wellington and Loxton. Map D

Laurel Glen Vineyard – Sonoma Valley Tasting Room – Wines: Cabernet Sauvignon, Rose, Sauvignon Blanc – 13750 Arnold Dr Suite #9, Glen Ellen, CA 95442 – www.laurelglen.com – Hours: Appointment. Grapes from Sonoma Mountain.

Lauterbach Cellars – Windsor – Wines: Syrah, Sparkling Pinot, Pinot Noir, Rose – 3420 Woolsey Road Windsor, CA 95492 – (707) 578-0537 – Hours: Appointment

Ledson Winery and Vineyards – Sonoma Valley – Grand Tasting Room – Wines: A wide variety – 7335 Highway 12 Santa Rosa CA 95409 – www.ledsonwinery.com – (707) 537-3810
Hours: 10:00am to 5:00pm – This is known locally as the 'castle', but it was originally built as a home and then became a tasting room and event space. It has a deli, spacious, rather austere tasting rooms and picnic tables for their items. They offer a wide variety of wines. They are at the top of the Sonoma Valley where it begins to flatten out on the way to Santa Rosa, so it makes a good place to stop for a tasting before heading south again. Map D

Limerick Lane Cellars – Russian River Valley – Off the Beaten Path Wines: Zinfandel, Syrah, Pinot Noir, Cabernet Sauvignon – 1023 Limerick Lane Healdsburg CA 95448 – www.limerick-lanewines.com – (707) 433-9211 – Hours: 10:00am to 5:00pm – This is a friendly, small winery founded by three friends. They make good wines and have a nice staff. The bottle shaped swimming pool is cool, not to make too obvious a pun. They are tucked over on Limerick Lane, safely off the beaten track, but worth a visit. Map E

Little Vineyards – Sonoma Valley – Wines: Zinfandel, Cabernet Sauvignon, Syrah – 15188 Sonoma Highway, Glen Ellen CA 95442 www.littlevineyards.com – (707) 996-2750 – Hours: 11:00am–5:00pm Thursday – Monday – This is a small, casual winery. The driveway is on the left–hand side (as you are heading north) just before the entrance for B.R. Cohn so it is convenient to the Sonoma Plaza. The tasting room/winery is surrounded by older vines. They have some outside seating in case you have packed a picnic. Map D

Littoral Wines – Russian River Valley – Wines: Chardonnays, Pinot Noirs – 788 Gold Ridge Road Sebastopol, CA 95472 – 707–823-9586 Hours: 9:00am to 5:00pm Monday – Sunday – info@littorai.com – This is a highly respected producer of Pinot Noir. The wine maker worked in France and the approach is biodynamic. The winery and vineyards are out of the way but they have an informative tour. Map E

Longboard Vineyards - Healdsburg – Surfer's Paradise – Wines: Syrah, Cabernet Sauvignon, Merlot – 5 Fitch St. Healdsburg CA 95448 www.longboardvineyards.com – (707) 433-3473 – Hours: 11:00am –7:00pm Thursday – Saturday, Sunday 11:00am–5:00pm – This is a tasting room and winery just a few minutes from the Healdsburg Plaza and nearby the Front Street Wineries. It was started by friends who share a love of surfing and the tasting room is decorated with surfboards and related photos. Map H

Loxton Cellars – Sonoma Valley – The Personal Touch – Wines: Rosé, Zinfandel, Syrah, Cabernet Sauvignon, Syrah Port, Chardonnay, Shiraz – 11466 Dunbar Rd. Glen Ellen CA 95442 – www.loxtoncellars.com – (707) 935-7221 – Hours: 11:00am–5:00pm – This is a small winery where Chris Loxton, the owner/winemaker is often pouring for you. As you enter, you walk past the winemaking equipment to reach the barrel room/tasting room. They have some nice, shaded picnic tables out front so bring a picnic. The entire staff is knowledgeable and friendly, partly because they don't just pour, they also make wine. Chris is from an Australian grape growing family, and a former physics professor, so his winemaking style is informed and unique. Visit during crush and you'll get your feet wet. No, you will not be stomping grapes, but the crush pad is in front of the building, so you are going to be walking through juice on the way to your tasting. The staff, including Chris, is almost always willing to chat about the process as they work. These are some great wines and they are only sold here! They also have one of the best Ports in the county. Chris has been doing a daily vineyard tour by appointment that is well worth taking. Map D

Lynmar Winery – Russian River Valley – Wines: Pinot Noir, Chardonnay, Vin Gris, Syrah – 9060 Frei Rd. Sebastopol CA 95472 – www.lynmarwinery.com – (707) 829-3374 – Hours: 10:00am–5:00pm Appointment – This is a jewel of a winery tucked into a lovely hollow to the south of the Russian River near to Olivet Road, and the cute town of Sebastopol. The winery has a wonderful ethic and that is shown in the architecture, great gardens and staff. They have a wonderful team of people working there. While you can taste standing up at the beautiful bar, most tastings take place at the tables inside or outside on the spacious patios. They have extensive organic, ornamental and vegetable gardens surrounding the tasting room. Beyond those, you see the hillsides of vines. When you look outside from the tasting bar, you can see the canopy that covers the winery in the distance on the top of the hill. The wines stand out and they have become well known for their Pinot Noir! Quite a few of their wines are from their own estate vineyards, but they also source grapes from other parts of the Russian River Valley and Coastal Sonoma. The biggest district in Sonoma is the Coastal AVA, which extends along the Pacific shoreline. Map E

MacRostie Winery and Vineyards – Russian River Valley – Wines: Rose, Chardonnay, Pinot Noir, Blends – 4605 Westside Road Healdsburg, CA 95448 – www.macrostiewinery.com – (707) 473-93038 – Hours: 11:00am–5:00pm Appointment – hospitality@macrostiewinery.com – This premium producer does their tasting in a lovely building perched on a hill in the Russian River Valley with wonderful views of the vines surrounding it. It is a seated tasting and they are very popular with a younger crowd so contact them well in advance. Map E

Manzanita Creek Winery – Healdsburg – Just Outside Downtown – Wines: Petite Syrah, Syrah, Zinfandel, Pinot Noir, Muscat – 1441–A Grove St. Healdsburg CA 95448 – www.manzanitacreek.com – (707) 433-4052 – Hours: 10:00am–5:00pm Wednesday – Saturday – They are in a light–industrial park on the edge of town. Of course, here industry means winemaking. They make good wines. Map H

Marimar Estate – Russian River Valley – Graton Road – Wines: Chardonnay, Pinot Noir, Syrah–Tempranillo – 11400 Graton Rd. Sebastopol CA 95472 – www.marimarestate.com – (707) 823-43658 – Hours: 11:00am–5:00pm Appointment – This charming winery is owned by a Spanish family with a long winemaking history. It is off by itself on Graton road on the way to the charming little town of Occidental. The building is classic Spain and the tasting is elegant. The road from there to Occidental is winding and there are no other well-known wineries immediately nearby so it probably limits their traffic. But the location is lovely and the wines are well–made. Map E

Martin Ray Winery –Russian River Valley – Look for the Water Tower – Wines: Pinot Gris, Sauvignon Blanc, Chardonnay,

Pinot Noir, Merlot, Cabernet Sauvignon, Gewürztraminer, Riesling – 2191 Laguna Rd. Santa Rosa CA 95401 – www.martinraywinery.com – (707) 823-2404 Hours: 11:00am–5:00pm Varies w/ Season – This is a cute winery that produces well-made, reasonably priced wines. The tasting is relaxed and may include a couple of their different labels. You can spot them as you approach because of their tall water tower looming over the road. The grounds are pretty and they have some nice picnic tables. The small tasting room has some interesting gifts and a nice, relaxed staff. If you are coming up from Guerneville Road, they are a bit farther than it looks like on the map. If you are reaching them from River Road going west, look for the Woodenhead Winery sign at the turn off. They are just down the road from the Joseph Swan Winery. Both Woodenhead and Joseph Swan make great stops. Map E

Martinelli Vineyards and Winery – Russian River Valley – Surprising Quality – Wines: Chardonnay, Pinot Noir, Syrah, Zinfandel, Gewürztraminer, Muscat Alexandria, Sauvignon Blanc – 3360 River Rd. Windsor CA 95965 – www.martinelliwinery.com – (707) 525-05708 – Hours: 10:00am–5:00pm – As you walk to this rustic building by the side of the road, you do not expect such a charming interior or such excellent wines. The family has been growing grapes alongside the Russian River and in Coastal Sonoma for many years. Their winery is located just a short distance off Highway 101 on River Road in a converted Hop Kiln building. It has fun, home style gifts and food items. They have a friendly and knowledgeable staff with picnic tables handy on the hillside and some deli items in a cooler. Map E

Martorana – Dry Creek Valley – Wines: Cabernet Sauvignon, Merlot, Zinfandel, Mozzafiato – 5956 W Dry Creek Rd, Healdsburg CA www.martoranafamilywinery.com – (707) 433-1909 – Hours: 11:00am–5:00pm – Appointment – info@martoranafamilywinery.com – A family run winery that has been farming vineyards in the area since the 1980's. Map F

Matanzas Creek Winery – Bennett Valley – Lavender and Wine – Wines: Merlot, Chardonnay, Sauvignon Blanc, Cabernet Sauvignon, Syrah, Rosé – 6097 Bennett Valley Rd. Santa Rosa CA 95404 – www.matanzascreek.com – (800) 590-6464 – Hours: 10:00am–4:30pm Tours – This medium sized winery is located about 15 minutes west of Glen Ellen along a narrow road that is a bit of a winding ride, but well worth the trip. It is a beautiful, Asian style building with lavender gardens, pretty grounds, great views and gifts. Not surprisingly, they also offer estate made lavender products along with their seriously good wines. Take the time to stroll through the lavender gardens, with their lovely views of the Bennett Valley. Inside the tasting room beyond the tasting bar, look at the educational displays. From here, you can either return to the Sonoma Valley or continue on Bennett Valley Road to Santa Rosa, Highway 101 and the Russian River Valley wineries. Map D

Matrix Winery – Russian River Valley on the Edge of Dry Creek – Wines: Chardonnay, Pinot Noir, Zinfandel, Syrah, Cabernet Sauvignon – 3291 Westside Rd. Healdsburg CA 95448 – www.matrixwinery.com – (707) 433-1911 – Hours: 11:00am–5:00pm – This is a small winery tucked on the western hillsides at the northern edge between the Russian River and Dry Creek regions. They have a cute, intimate tasting room with nice views, and they are conveniently located. Their wines are nicely made from grapes from Alexander Valley, Russian River, Sonoma Coast and Dry Creek areas with an appeal to collectors. The winemaker pays a lot of attention to classic methods and the exact barrels for aging each varietal. Map E

Mauritson Family Winery – Dry Creek Valley – Rock Pile – Wines: Chardonnay, Zinfandel, Cabernet Sauvignon, Sauvignon Blanc, Syrah, Petite Syrah – 2859 Dry Creek Rd. Healdsburg CA 95448 – www.mauritsonwines.com – (707) 431-0804 Hours: 10:00am–5:00pm Appointment – This family has been growing grapes in this area since the 1860's when all of their wine was sent home to Sweden. Much of their original vineyards are now under water as part of Lake Sonoma, developed by the state in the 1960's. Today they have their vines on the dramatic ridges overlooking the lake in one of the county's newest AVA's called Rock Pile. This area is known for wonderful wines and it comes with a lot of effort. Some of the family vineyards are so steep and rough that everything has to be done by hand, no tractors. Fortunately, the tasting room is conveniently located at the intersection of Dry Creek Road and Lytton Springs Road, just two minutes from the Dry Creek General Store and ten minutes from downtown Healdsburg. They have a friendly, nicely decorated tasting room with tables and umbrellas outside. There are so few wineries that feature the wonderful grapes of Rockpile that it would be worth visiting here just for that reason. Hint: Visit earlier in the day since the western facing entranceway fills the tasting room with bright, afternoon sunlight and it can be a little overwhelming. Map F

Mayo Family Winery – Sonoma Valley – Wines: A Very Wide Variety – 13101 Arnold Dr. Glen Ellen CA 95442 – www.mayofamilywinery.com – (707) 938-9401 – Hours: 10:00am–6:30pm – They have two locations. This address in Glen Ellen is their main winery and tasting room offering their larger line of wines in a casual environment. It is located where Arnold Drive meets Highway 12. Their reserve room is located across from the Kenwood Winery. Although the name sounds Irish, the family is from France; the name was changed upon their arrival in the States. The winery tasting room is spacious where they feature well-made, reasonably priced wines. As a result, they tend to attract a younger crowd, which makes the place a lot of fun. Their reserve room in Kenwood is more intimate. Map D

Mayo Family Reserve – Sonoma Valley – Food Pairings – Wines: Chardonnay, Viognier, Zinfandel, Petite Syrah, Cabernet Sauvignon, Cabernet Franc, Zinfandel Port – 9200 Sonoma Highway Kenwood CA 95452 – www.mayofamilywinery.com – (707) 833-5504 – Hours: 10:00am–6:30pm – In their reserve room they do food pairings. They are next to VJB. It is a more expensive tasting than at the other, but fun. Calling it 'a 'food pairing' understates the experience. This is a pairing menu of seven courses, each with its own wine from their reserve list, created by their Executive Chef. It is a considerable amount of food and wine and not to be rushed. Map D

Mazzocco Vineyards – Dry Creek Valley near Alexander Valley – Wines: Chardonnay, Viognier, Carignane, Pinot Noir, Zinfandel, Cabernet Sauvignon, Merlot, Blends – 1400 Lytton Springs Rd. Healdsburg CA 95448 – www.mazzocco.com – (707) 431-8159 – Hours: 11:00am–5:00pm – This is a pretty winery perched up on a rise near the small local airport. The original winery owner lived in LA and liked the spot because he could fly up in his plane and walk next door. They make some great Chardonnay and Rhone–style wines. The tasting room is bright and airy with lovely views of the vineyards and a nice staff. It is currently owned by the Wilsons who have several wineries. It is a good stop between Dry Creek and Alexander valleys. Map F

Meadowcroft Wines – Sonoma Valley – At the Cornerstone Center Wines: Blanc de Blanc, French Colombard, Sauvignon Blanc, Chardonnay, Pinot Noir, Zinfandel, Syrah, Cabernet Sauvignon – 23574 Arnold Drive, Sonoma, CA 95476 – www.meadowcroftwines.com – (707) 934-4090 – Hours: 12:00pm to 4:00pm – Appointment. Map B

Meeker Vineyards – Alexander Valley – Tasting Room – Wines: Bordeaux, Cabernet Sauvignon, Merlot, Zinfandel, Petite Syrah, Syrah, Carignane, Ice wine – 5 Fitch St Unit B, Healdsburg, CA 95448 www.meekervineyards.com – (707) 431-2148 – Hours: 11:00am–4:00pm. Map G

Merriam Vineyards – On the Southern Edge of Healdsburg and Windsor – Wines: Bordeaux, Chardonnay – 11650 Los Amigos Road, Healdsburg, California 95448 – www.MerriamVineyards.com – (707) 433-4032 – Hours: 10:00am to 5:00pm. Map E

Merry Edwards – Russian River Valley – Well Respected– Wines: Pinot Noir, Sauvignon Blanc, Chardonnay – 2959 Gravenstein Highway North, Sebastopol, CA 95472 – www.merryedwards.com – (707) 823-7466 – Hours: 9:30–4:30 Appointment – This is a premier maker of Pinot Noir. They do both a bar and a lovely seated tasting and the wines are wonderful, the staff is friendly and knowledgeable and the place is appealing. The wines are not inexpensive. Their Sauvignon Blanc has received the highest scores ever awarded to an American Sauvignon Blanc, made from grapes grown in this valley where general wisdom says it could not be done. Map E

Michel-Schlumberger Wine Estate – Dry Creek Valley – Wines: Cabernet Sauvignon, Syrah, Pinot Noir, Merlot, Pinot Blanc, Chardonnay 4155 Wine Creek Rd. Healdsburg CA 95448 – www.michelschlumberger.com – (707) 433-7427 – Hours: 11:00am–5:00pm Appointment – This is a pretty winery in a classic building surrounding a courtyard, on a side road off of West Dry Creek Road. It has a European feel to the place, and the tasting areas make you feel like you're in a charming French home. They are by appointment. Our experience with them has always been pleasant. The only other winery on the same road is Mounts Family Winery, a small family place with a distinctly rustic tasting experience surrounded by vineyards. Map F

Mietz Cellars – Russian River Valley – Wines: Zinfandel, Sauvignon Blanc, Chardonnay, Merlot, Pinot Noir – 602 Limerick Lane Healdsburg, CA 95448 – www.mietzcellars.com – (707) 433-7103 – Hours: Appointment. Map E

Mill Creek Vineyards and Winery – The Edge of Dry Creek Valley by Russian River Valley – A Family Affair – Wines: Chardonnay, Syrah, Gewürztraminer, Sauvignon Blanc, Zinfandel – 1401 Westside Rd. Healdsburg CA 95448 – www.millcreekwinery.com – (707) 431-2121 Hours: 10:00am to 5:00pm – Seven members of the Kreck family make this place work from vineyard to bottle to shelf. They farm fifty plus acres of their own vines at the southern edge of the Dry Creek Valley, then make the wine and market it. They have a nice middle of the road price point that makes it easier to take some wine home with you. The tasting room is patterned on the Mills that were once common in the area, and the property includes a water wheel and mill pond. They have two large picnic areas and the tasting room is made mostly of local Redwood. Not surprisingly, their wine club is called the Sequoia Club. If you want to picnic with a larger group you should call them in advance. Map F

Mountain Terraces Winery and Vineyards – Sonoma Valley in the Hills – Wines: Cabernet Sauvignon – 3030 Cavedale Road Glen Ellen, CA 95442 – Not Currently Seeing visitors probably due to problems with the road – www.mountainterraces.com – (707) 996-1787 – info@mountainterraces.com. Map D

Mounts Family Winery – Dry Creek – Wines: Zinfandel, Petite Syrah, Cabernet Sauvignon, Cabernet Franc – 3901 Wine Creek Rd Healdsburg CA 95448 – www.mountswinery.com – (707) 292-8148 – Hours: Weekends and Appointment – The family has farmed these gorgeous hills on the west side of the Dry Creek Valley since the 1940's, and they are still a farming family, but now they are winemakers too. The winery is on site and the tasting room/barrel room is a low roofed workroom attached to a barn, but while the location is rustic, the views are great and the man who makes the wine pours it for you. The wines are well–made and the Petite Syrah stands out. When they are open to the public they put a sign up at the intersection of West Dry Creek Road and Wine Creek Road. Just past them on the same road is Michel–Schlumberger. Map F

Murphy-Goode Estate Vineyard and Winery –Downtown Healdsburg Tasting Room – Wines: Fumé Blanc, Chardonnay, Cabernet Sauvignon, Merlot, Pinot Noir, Zinfandel, Claret, Petit Verdot, Rosé, Muscat Canelli – 20 Matheson St. Healdsburg CA 95448 – www.murphygoodewinery.com – (707) 431-7644 – Hours: 10:30–5:30 – The tasting room is located just across the street from the Healdsburg Plaza. It is a spacious place with a nice tasting bar. The wines are well made. The vineyards and winery are in the central part of the Alexander Valley.

Muscardini Cellars – Sonoma Valley – Tasting Room – Wines: Rosato di Sangiovese, Zinfandel, Barbera, Syrah, Cabernet Sauvignon – 8910 Sonoma Highway Kenwood CA 95452 – www.muscardinicellars.com – (707) 933-9305 – Hours: 11:00am–6:00pm – The wines are good examples of how much microclimates and grape selections can create unique and delicious results. The wines are well-made and full of that lovely Sonoma Valley depth and complexity. The tasting room is roomy with a large sitting porch out front and plenty of parking.

Mutt Lynch Winery – Windsor – Wines: Chardonnay, Rose, Cabernet Sauvignon, Merlot – 9050 Windsor Road Windsor, CA 95492 – www.muttlynchwinery.com– (707) 687-5089 – Hours: 11:00am–6:00pm Appointment – Very Dog Friendly.

Nalle Winery – Dry Creek Valley – Grass Covered Tasting Room – Wines: Zinfandel, Pinot Noir, Sauvignon Blanc, Chardonnay 2383 Dry Creek Rd. Healdsburg CA 95448 – www.nallewinery.com – (707) 433-1040 – Hours: 12–5 Saturday and other days by Appointment – This is a small winery that is covered with grass, and it is a lot more interesting looking on the outside than inside. They make interesting wines, but they are open on a rather irregular schedule. They have a small case production and sell out quickly. Map F

Nicholson Ranch – Southern Sonoma Valley on the edge of Los Carneros – Great Views – Wines: Chardonnay, Pinot, Syrah – 4200 Napa Rd. Sonoma CA 95476 – www.nicholsonranch.com – (707) 938-8822 – Hours: 10:00am–6:00pm – They are located at the intersection of Napa Road (that takes you into downtown Sonoma) and Route 121. It sits on top of their caves and they have picnic tables alongside their pond. There are nice views from the grounds, although unfortunately you don't enjoy the views from the tasting room which is at the back of the building. It seems like they should be in the Los Carneros District rather than Sonoma Valley, but that area is just south of them, across the road. Being at that nexus of roads and districts must be rather confusing, because the wines they make have more in common with Los Carneros than the Sonoma Valley. They periodically do tours of their caves for groups. The property has livestock including Llamas and a Temple to Aphrodite. Map B

Notre Vue Estate and Balverne Winery – Windsor – Wines: Pinot Noir, Sauvignon Blanc, Chardonnay – 11010 Estate Lane Windsor, CA 95492 – www.notrevueestate.com – Hours: 10:30am to 4:30pm – (707) 433-4050.

Old World Winery – Russian River Valley – Wines: Abundance, Luminous, Flow, Era, Bouschet – 850 River Road Fulton, CA 95439 www.oldworldwinery.com – (707) 490-6696 – Hours: 11:00am–5:00pm Appointment. A small winery on the south side of River Road not far from Highway 101. Map E

Optima Winery – Dry Creek Valley in the Timber Crest Center – Wines: Rose, Gewurztraminer, Zinfandel, Petite Syrah, Cabernet Sauvignon – 4791 Dry Creek Road Healdsburg, CA 95448 – www.optimawinery.com – (707) 431-8222 – Hours: 10:30am to 4:30pm – Appointment. Map F

Orsi Family Vineyards – Southside of Downtown Healdburg – Opened 2021 in Healdsburg – 2306 Magnolia Dr. Healdsburg CA 95448 – www.orsifamilyvineyards.com – (707) 732-4660 Hours: 10:30-4:30 – The Orsi family owns vineyards in various North Bay regions and this is the first time that they have their own tasting room. They are located across Highway 101 from downtown Healdsburg. They specialize in Italian wine grape varieties including biancolella, schioppettino and negroamaro along with better-known sangiovese, montepulciano and primitivo. They also make the classica California varietals. Map E

Pangloss Cellars – Downtown Sonoma Tasting – Wines: Rose, Sauvignon Blanc, Genache, Chardonnay, Pinot Noir, Zinfandel, Syrah, Cabernet Sauvignon – 35 E Napa St, Sonoma, CA 95476 – www.panglosscellars.com – (707) 933-8565 – They offer a private, focused, immersive seated tasting accompanied by a local cheese and charcuterie plate for each guest. Hours: 11:00am to 2:00pm – Appointment.

Papapietro Perry – Dry Creek Valley in the Timber Crest Center – Popular Pinot – Wines: Pinot Noir, Zinfandel – 4791 Dry Creek Rd. Healdsburg CA 95448 – www.papapietroperry.com – (707) 433-0422 – Hours: 11:00am–4:00pm – They are known for their great wines, and it is a surprisingly small, low key tasting room considering the enthusiasm of their loyal clientele. But it is a fun tasting room. They are walking distance to Kokomo, Amphora and Peterson Wineries so you can stroll and taste. Map F

Paradise Ridge – Santa Rosa Hills with Views – 4545 Thomas Lake Harris Dr. Santa Rosa CA 95403 – www.prwinery.com – (707) 528-9463 – Hours: 11:00am–5:00pm – This winery sits at the crest of a hill overlooking Santa Rosa. The wines are good, and it sits amid a sculpture garden. There are few other wineries in this area, although across Highway 101 there are some wineries in the nearby corporate park, and beyond that, the wineries on the southern edges of the Russian River. Map E

Passagio Wines – www.passaggiowines.com – Their downtown Sonoma Tasting Room closed but they are still making wine.

Passalacqua Winery – Dry Creek Valley – Charming and Friendlyy – Wines: Sauvignon Blanc, Chardonnay, Zinfandel, Cabernet Sauvignon, Sangiovese, Primitivo – 3805 Lambert Bridge Rd. Healdsburg CA 95448 – www.passalacquawinery.com – (707) 433-5550 – Hours: 11:00am–5:00pm – This is a small, family winery at the heart of the Dry Creek Valley in sight of the General Store. They make elegant wines poured in a well-lit, friendly tasting room with views of the valley. This is a family run winery, and the Passalacqua family has a long history here. Their own vineyards are farther south in the valley, and for the rest, they source their grapes from diverse areas, resulting in a interesting collection. The winery is just across from the tasting room, and being tight on space, the winemaking often spreads out into the walkway between the two buildings. They are located across the street from the Dry Creek Winery. Map F

Patz and Hall – South of the Sonoma Plaza – Wines: Chardonnay, Pinot Noir, Sparkling – 21200 8th St E, Sonoma, CA 95476 – www.patzhall.com (707) 265-7700 – Hours: Appointment – This is a premium Pinot producer that sources grapes from a number of regions. They do a lovely seated tasting, often on the back patio with views of the region. Map B

Paul Hobbs – Russian River Valley – Wines: Chardonnay, Cabernet Sauvignon, Cabernet Franc – 3355 Gravenstein Highway N, Sebastopol, CA 95472 – www.paulhobbswinery.com – (707) 824-9879 Hours: 10:00am to 2:00pm – Appointment – The owner is one of America's most significant consulting winemakers, and this is his home winery, where he offers his best. This is a fancy, seated tasting for the collector. Map E

Paul Mathew – Tasting Room – Russian River Valley – Wines: Grenache, Pinot Noir, Cabernet Franc, Gewurtraminer, Rose – 9060 Graton Road Graton, CA 95444 – (707) 861-9729 – Hours: 10:30am to 4:30pm – www.paulmathewvineyards.com. They are located in the little Graton downtown. Map E

Pech Merle Winery – Alexander Valley Tasting Room – Wines: Rose de Syrah, Sauvignon Blanc, Viognier, Pinot Noir, Zinfandel, Carignan 21001 Geyserville Ave, Geyserville CA 95441 – www.pechmerlewinery.com – (707) 891-3015 – Hours: 11:00am–6:00pm – Appointment.

Pedroncelli Winery – Dry Creek Original – Wines: Sauvignon Blanc, Chardonnay, Sangiovese, Merlot, Zinfandel, Cabernet Sauvignon, Syrah, Petite Syrah, Port – 1220 Canyon Rd. Geyserville CA 95441 – www.pedroncelli.com – (800) 836-3894 – Hours: 10:00am–4:30pm – The vineyards have been in this family since 1927 and this is the oldest tasting room in the Dry Creek Valley. Of course, saying they are in the Valley does not describe their location because Canyon Road is one of the connections between the Dry Creek and Alexander Valleys. They offer a wide variety of wines well suited to this area. During prohibition, they supplied home winemakers with grapes. While you could not sell wine, you could still make a limited amount for personal use and the Italian community was an especially good market for grape growers. The wines are from a mix of vines planted a hundred years ago and recently replanted vineyards. The tasting room is relaxed and pleasant. They feature the work of local artists. Map F

Pellegrini Family Vineyards – Russian River Valley – Italian Family Tradition – Wines: Pinot Noir, Chardonnay, Cabernet Sauvignon, Merlot, Rosato, Carignane, Sauvignon Blanc, Zinfandel – 4055 W. Olivet Rd. Santa Rosa CA 95401 – ww.pellegrinisonoma.com – (707) 575-8465 – Hours: 10:30–4:30 – This big blocky, Italian style building towers over the surrounding vineyards and the tasting inside was at a small bar in the barrel room, but it may have changed. The design supports production over hospitality, but the wines are well–made. They are around the corner from the wineries of Olivet Road, including DeLoach and Hook and Ladder. Nearby are Lynmar and Ironhorse. Map E

Peterson Family Winery – Dry Creek Valley at the Timber Crest Center – Wines: Zinfandel, Cabernet Sauvignon, Petite Syrah, Sangiovese, Syrah, Muscat Blanc, Carignane Blend – 4791 Dry Creek Rd. Bldg. #7 Healdsburg CA 95448 – www.petersonwinery.com – (707) 431-7568 Hours: 11:00am–4:00pm – This is a pleasant, spacious tasting room with good wines just steps from

Amphora and Kokomo. They have a pleasant staff and a pretty, well-lit tasting room. Map F

Petroni Vineyards – Sonoma Valley Hills – Closed. Map D

Pezzi King Vineyards – Downtown Healdsburg – Tasting Room – Wines: Chardonnay, Zinfandel, Merlot, Cabernet Sauvignon – 412 Hudson Street Healdsburg 95448 – www.pezziking.com – (707) 431-9388 – Hours: 10:00am–5:00pm – This winery has a long history in the Dry Creek Valley and currently has their offices and tasting room near the Front Street Wineries. Map H

Portalupi Wine – Downtown Healdsburg – Tasting Room – Wines: Graziano, Syrah, Primitivo, Pinot Noir, Verminti-no, Arneis, Zinfandel, Petite Sirah, Charbono – 107 North St, Healdsburg, CA 95448 – www.portalupiwine.com – (707) 395-0960 – Hours:11:00am to 7:00pm – Appointment. Map H

Porter Creek Vineyards – Russian River Valley – River Edge Wines: Chardonnay, Viognier, Pinot Noir, Syrah, Carignane – 8735 Westside Rd. Healdsburg CA 95448 – www.porter-creekvineyards.com – (707) 433-6321 – Hours: 11:00am–4:00pm – This is a small family run winery in a charming, traditional tasting room at the southern edge of Westside Road. They are nested amid Redwood trees and Oak trees just north of the Russian River. The wines are good and range from medium to moderately expensive. Their vineyards are Biodynamic and Organic. They are nearby the Gary Farrell Winery. Map F

Preston of Dry Creek – Organic Vineyards – Wines: Petite Syrah, Syrah, Sauvignon Blanc, Barbera, Mourvèdre, Cinsault, Carignane, Rousanne, Viognier, Vin Gris, Blends, Olive Oil, Olives – 9282 W. Dry Creek Rd. Healdsburg CA 95448 – www.prestonofdrycreek.com – (707) 433-3372 – Hours: 11:00am–4:00pm – This winery started off on a more conventional path with chemicals and larger production, and then Preston dramatically changed directions, reducing production and converting the vineyards to organic. You reach the winery via a gravel road at the top of the valley and the feeling of the place is authentic Dry Creek, with a welcoming garden complete with tables and shade. In true country style, the winery also has a bakery, olive oil samples and gracious grounds that make a relaxed, friendly experience. This is a great place to bring a picnic. Both their olive oil and their wines are good. They are around the corner from Ferrari Carano, nearby Zichichi and Bella wineries. Map F

Quivira Vineyards – Dry River Valley – High Tech Dry Creek – Wines: Zinfandel, Sauvignon Blanc, Syrah, Petite Syrah, Grenache, Rhone blends – 4900 W. Dry Creek Rd. Healdsburg CA 95448 – www.quivirawine.com – (707) 431-8333 – Hours: 11:00am–5:00pm – This is a Biodynamic/Organic winery with 'green' buildings. Surrounding the winery are vegetable gardens, chicken coops, pigs and goats. The roof is covered in solar panels. Between the gardens and the panels it looks like a science project gone wild, but they make good wines and do a fun tasting. Quivira was the name of a mythical Chinese city thought to be located on California's North Coast by the Spanish sailors who first explored the area. Why did they think that? Because they saw Chinese Junks sailing the coast when they first arrived! They were probably seeing stranded sailors from the great Chinese treasure fleets that sailed this coast in the early 1400's. After all, some of them were shipwrights so it's no surprise that they would build boats. The original owner collected maps of Quivira, and there was a gallery room displaying the maps. But when the winery was sold to the present owners the maps left, although the name remained. The hospitality tends to be variable; maybe the design of the building promotes a certain amount of eccentricity but it is a fun experience. Map F

Ram's Gate Winery – Los Carneros – Wines: Sauvignon Blanc, Chardonnay, Pinot Noir, Syrah, Cabernet Sauvignon – 28700 Arnold Dr, Sonoma, CA 95476 – www.ramsgatewinery.com – (707) 721-8700 – Hours: 11:00am–6:00pm – Appointment – This is an elegant winery that greets visitors as they arrive in

Los Carneros from San Francisco. It has the feeling of a restaurant and bar with views. Map B

Ramazzotti Wines – Alexander Valley Tasting Room – Wines: Sparkling Rose, Frizzante Brut, Blanc de Blanc, Sauvignon Blanc, Pinot Grigio, Chardonnay, Zinfandel Rose, Barbera, Sangiovese, Cabernet Sauvignon – 21015 Geyserville Ave, Geyserville CA 95441 – www.ramazzottiwines.com – (707) 814-0016 – Hours: 11:00am–5:00pm. Map G

Raymond Burr Vineyards – Dry Creek Valley – An Actor's Vineyard – Wines: Cabernet Sauvignon, Cabernet Franc, Chardonnay – 8339 W. Dry Creek Rd. Healdsburg CA 95448 – www.raymondburrvineyards.com – (707) 433-8559 – Hours: 10:00am–5:00pm Appointment – This is a small, by appointment winery that was founded by the famous actor. They do tours of their orchids by appointment on Saturdays. It is informal and relaxed, at the upper edges of the valley. Map F

Red Car Wine – Russian River Valley Tasting Room – Wines: Chardonnay, Pinot Noir, Syrah – 8400 Graton Road Sebastopol, CA 95472 – www.redcarwine.com – (707) 829-8500 – Hours: 10:00am to 5:00pm – Appointment. Map E

Reeve Wines – Alexander Valley – Wines: Pinot Noir, Prism Riesling, Vermentino, Grenache, Chardonnay – 4551 Dry Creek Road Healdsburg, CA 95448 – www.reevewines.com – (707) 235-6345 – Hours: 11:00am–5:00pm – Appointment – This is a charming family winery, tucked up on the eastern hills of the valley. The tasting is typically outside if weather permits and this area has great weather. Map G

Reprise Winery – Sonoma Valley Hills – Wines: A Variety –1700 Moon Mountain Road Sonoma, CA 95476 – www.repriswines.com (707) 931-7701 – Hours: 11:00am–5:00pm – Appointment – This sits on top of Moon Mountain to the north of the Sonoma Plaza. It is a narrow ride up there but you pass the famous Monte Rossa vineyards, known for its red soil. It is a beautiful location that sits in a bowl surrounded by the mountains. They do a tour of the hill top property in an ATV as part of the tasting and the wines tend to be on the lighter side with a couple of exceptions. Map D

Ridge Lytton Springs – Russian River Valley on the edge of the Alexander Valley – Big Zinfandels – Wines: Cabernet Sauvignon, Zinfandel, Grenache – 650 Lytton Springs Rd. Healdsburg CA 95448 – www.ridgewine.com – (707) 433-7721 – Hours: 11:00am–4:00pm – This is the northern branch of the well–respected Ridge Winery. Behind the stunning, modern building is acres of old vine Zinfandel, Petite Syrah, Alicante Bouschet and more. The tasting is fun and relaxed with views of the rolling hills filled with old vines. The wines deserve their great reputation. Ridge was one of the wines chosen to compete in the 1976 Judgment of Paris, although it did not win. But here is an interesting addition to the story. The movie Bottle Shock (2008) tells the story of the competition, and parts of it were filmed in downtown Sonoma. When the movie opened they staged a repeat of the competition including the original wineries. This time Ridge won! They have some of the largest organic vineyards in Sonoma. Lytton Springs Road connects the Dry Creek Valley to the Alexander Valley, so this makes a great tasting stop as you travel from one valley to the other. Map F

Robert Young Estate Winery – Alexander – Famous Chardonnay from Alexander Valley – Wines: Chardonnay, Merlot, Cabernet Sauvignon, Cabernet Franc, Blends – 4960 Red Winery Rd. Geyserville CA 95441 – www.ryew.com – (707) 431-4811 – Hours: 10:00am–4:30pm– This is a wonderful winery with a hilltop tasting room that overlooks the valley. It sits on the eastern side of Alexander Valley. Most of their grapes are sold to other premium producers, most notably Chateau St. Jean, but what they make for themselves is good. It is a charming experience in a great location. Map G

Robledo Family Winery – Southwest Sonoma Valley on the edge of Los Carneros – Down Home Friendly – Wines: Chardonnay, Pinot Grigio, Moscato, Cabernet Sauvignon, Merlot, Pinot Noir, Pinot Blanc, Sauvignon Blanc. 21901 Bonness Rd. Sonoma CA 95476 – www.robledofamilywinery.com – (707) 939-6903 – Hours: 10:00am–5:00pm, Sunday until 4:00pm by Appointment. The Robledo family is a large clan and they make great wines. The tasting room is down–home friendly and always worth a visit. During the Passport weekends, when wineries are open to anyone who has purchased a pass and a glass, this is the one of our favorite places to visit. The wines are good and a real value. The Robledo family and their story is an important part of the fabric that makes Sonoma special. The tasting/barrel room is comfortable and spacious with large tables and a tasting bar where they display their many ribbons. They are nearby to Roche Family, the next listing. Map B

Roche Winery and Vineyards – Sonoma Valley – At the Plaza and the Estate – Wines: Chardonnay, Pinot Noir, Merlot, Syrah, Cabernet Sauvignon, Muscat Cannelli, Tamarix blend of Chardonnay, Syrah and Pinot Noir – At the Plaza – 122 West Spain St. Sonoma CA 95476 – At the Winery – 22097A Bonness Rd, Sonoma, CA – 95476 www.rochewinery.com – (800) 825-9475 – Hours: Check the website for the two locations – This long time Los Carneros grower has a lovely winery in the southeast corner of the Sonoma Valley just north of the Los Carneros line. They also have a tasting room at the northeast corner of the Sonoma plaza in a charming little craftsman style bungalow. They make wonderful, properly priced wines and they have a friendly staff. In the nicer weather, which is the norm here, they have an outdoor tastings. The Plaza tasting room is next door to 'the Girl and the Fig' restaurant. Map B

Rodney Strong Vineyards – Russian River Valley – A Unique Building – Wines: Sauvignon Blanc, Chardonnay, Pinot Noir, Merlot, Syrah, Cabernet Sauvignon, Meritage, Zinfandel, Port – 11455 Old Redwood Highway. Healdsburg CA 95448 –

www.rodneystrong.com – (707) 433-6511 – Hours: 10:00am–5:00pm – This is a unique wooden building with a cool self-tour where you walk around the perimeter and look down on the various tanks. There is a great story that goes along with the winery, and that is what you will see depicted on the walls as part of the tour. This is a relatively large winery for this area. Rodney Strong was a song and dance man who, together with his wife, started in the wine business in a funny way. They would come up to this area, buy wine, take it back to their home, and blend it. They lived by a yacht club and they would sell the wine from their home. Rodney decided that he could not be an old song and dance man, but he could be an old winemaker, so they bought their first vineyard in Sonoma and the rest is history. Today the winery is owned by another family, but the reputation of Rodney Strong continues. They make good, solid wines poured in a interesting tasting room suspended above the winery. They have a nice gift section and are located on the same driveway as the J Winery, and the location is convenient to both Highway 101 and Healdsburg. Map E

Roth Estate Winery – Russian River Valley Chalk Hill – Wines: Cabernet Sauvignon, Syrah, Pinot Noir, Chardonnay, Merlot – 10309 Chalk Hill Road Healdsburg, CA 95448 – ww.www.rothwinery.com – (707) 836-7030 – Hours: 11:00am–5:00pm – Appointment – concierge@rothwinery.com – This sits across the road from the Chalk Hill Winery and it is owned by the same people. It is a fun, popular place, although the drive to both places requires a great number of turns. Map E

Rued Winery – Dry Creek Valley – Six Generations – Wines: Chardonnay, Sauvignon Blanc, Zinfandel, Cabernet Sauvignon – 3850 Dry Creek Road Healdsburg, CA 95448 – www.ruedvineyards.com – (707) 433-3261 – Hours: 11:00am–4:00pm This family has been farming in Sonoma for 125 years and six generations, but this is actually a new tasting room, conveniently located just up the road from the Dry Creek Store. It is charming, the staff is knowledgeable and Northern Sonoma friendly and the wines are good. Being a newer winery, the price point is good, and the views of the valley are lovely. It is nearby Truett Hurst and the Timber Crest Center and Unti. Map F

Russian Hill Estate Winery – Russian River Valley – Great Views in Russian River Valley – Wines: Pinot Noir, Syrah, Chardonnay, Port – 4525 Slusser Rd. Windsor CA 95452 – www.russianhillestate.com – (707) 575-9428 – Hours: 10:00am–4:00pm Thursday to Monday – This pretty winery sits behind the Santa Rosa Airport. When you are in the tasting room, or enjoying the patio out back, the views of the rolling hills are great. They are just north of the well-known Sonoma Cutrer Winery, and you can see the restored Hop Kiln building which is part of Sonoma Cutrer's operations. They have nice wines, a good, relaxed staff and a nice tasting experience off the beaten path. Map E

Saint Anne's Crossing – Sonoma Valley – Wines: Zinfandel, Cabernet Sauvignon, Malbec, Petite Verdot – 8450 Sonoma Highway, Kenwood, CA 95452 – www.stannescrossing.com – (707) 598-5200 – Hours: 11:00am–5:00pm – It was started by the Wilsons to feature Dry Creek Zinfandel, but over the years it has stretched out a bit. This is a pretty tasting room, that sits in front of the winery. It has a nice patio out back. It is across the street from Chateau St. Jean. Map D

Saint Francis Vineyard and Winery – The Top of the Sonoma Valley – Wines: Chardonnay, Cabernet Sauvignon, Merlot, Zinfandel, Syrah – 100 Pythian Rd. Santa Rosa CA 95409 – www.st-franciswine.com – (888) 675-9463 – Hours: 10:00am–5:00pm – The tasting room is a dramatic Spanish style visitor's center that was designed to take advantage of the wonderful views of their vineyards and the mountains in the distance. You can see the separate winery building tucked against the mountains at the back of the property. The traffic light at the intersection of Highway 12 and Pythian Road makes it a great 'northern limit' for a Sonoma Valley tour on a busy day. Whenever you can make it easy and safe to turn around, you should take advantage of that. The tasting room is spacious, with a long tasting bar and a nice gift area. The staff is pleasant and there are lovely patios and grounds, including covered areas to sit and chat. They also do wonderful seated food pairings by appointment. Map D

Sangiacomo Wines – Sonoma Valley – A long time Los Carneros Grower – Pinot Noir, Chardonnay – 21545 Broadway, Sonoma CA 21545 – sangiacomowines.com – (707) 934-8445 – Hours: Appointment – The tasting is at their ranch just off Broadway south of the Sonoma Plaza. The family has been growing grapes for local wineries for many years, and finally they decided to use some of the grapes for their own label. Map B

Sbragia Family Vineyards – Dry Creek Valley – Great Views – Wines: Sauvignon Blanc, Chardonnay, Merlot, Zinfandel, Cabernet Sauvignon – 9990 Dry Creek Rd Geyserville CA 95441 – www.sbragia.com – (707) 473-2992 – Hours: 11:00am–5:00pm – This dramatic winery is perched on a hillside at the north end of the Dry Creek Valley across from the dam that formed Lake Sonoma and it has the best views of any winery in the valley. On the maps, this looks farther than it is, but it is just five minutes north of the popular Ferrari–Carano winery. It is worth a visit, being family owned and run, the hospitality is good. Ed Sbragia was the head winemaker at Beringer for many years and his sure hand is evident in this wonderful collection of wines. They do tastings both inside at the bar and sitting outside on the spacious patio. They offer reserve tastings for the enthusiast on the weekend, in a small, charming building called the Ark. Map F

Scribe Winery – Southern Sonoma Valley on the edge of Los Carneros – Wines: Rose, Chardonnay, Pinot Noir, Syrah, Cabernet Sauvignon – 2100 Denmark St, Sonoma, CA 95476 – (707) 939-1858 – Hours: 11:30am to 4:00pm – Appointment – They are located on the hillsides south of the Sonoma Plaza, just north of the Los Carneros line. They have two sites for tasting, a casual hillside with blankets to sit on the grass for the wine club members, and a restored white house that they use for general tasting that can be seen from Napa Road. It is very popular with a younger crowd. Map B

Schug Carneros Estate Winery – Los Carneros – Views and Pinot – Wines: Sauvignon Blanc, Chardonnay, Pinot Noir, Merlot, Cabernet Franc, Cabernet Sauvignon, Syrah, Blanc de Noirs Sparkling Pinot Noir – 602 Bonneau Rd. Sonoma CA 95476 – www.schugwinery.com – (707) 939-9363 – Hours: 10:00am–5:00pm – They are a Carneros Estate Winery, wonderfully convenient to San Francisco. Many of their grapes grow on the gorgeous hillsides right outside the charming tasting room door. They have a knowledgeable staff, with excellent wines and a great, German-style building. Schug was the founding winemaker at the revered Joseph Phelps Winery in Napa, and was involved in the production of Napa's first Bordeaux blend. However, his love of Burgundy wines, Pinot Noir and Chardonnay, led him to open his own winery in this pretty canyon. The wines are well–made and a good deal. They do tours by appointment. They have great views of Carneros, and the Bay and they are just minutes from Gloria Ferrer, Jacuzzi, Cline & Roche. Map B

Sebastiani Vineyards and Winery – Downtown Sonoma – A Long Tradition – Wines: Cabernet Sauvignon, Merlot, Barbera, Zinfandel, Pinot Noir – 389 – 4th St. E. Sonoma CA 95476 – www.sebastiani.com – (707) 938-5532 – Hours: 10:00am–5:00pm – This old time Sonoma winery is near the Sonoma Plaza. In the 1990's, they sold their bulk wine division and began concentrating on premium wines, producing high–quality, reasonably–priced wines. Take the time to visit the historic barrel room that use for events inside the beautiful visitor center. The Sebastiani Winery opened for business in 1906. They were able to operate through prohibition because Samuele got a permit to make sacramental wine for the churches. Even though they were closely monitored by the government, they didn't know that he had buried tanks and special valves in the winery. After making the approved volume of wine, when the revenue official left, he would sent the wine into these hidden tanks and make more. By the time Prohibition finished he had hundreds of thousands of gallons of wine aging in the cool tanks underground. The family sold the winery in 2009, however members of the family continue in the wine business, and own vineyards and wineries in the area. Map B

Seghesio Winery – Healdsburg – Traditional Healdsburg – Wines: Zinfandel, Arneis, Pinot Grigio, Barbera, Sangiovese, Italian varietals – 14730 Grove St. Healdsburg CA 95448 – www.seghesio.com – (707) 433-3579 – Hours: 10:00am–5:00pm – The winery is located five minutes from the plaza in downtown Healdsburg; the town simply grew up around them. They planted their first vineyards in 1895, and they continue to make good solid wines. The winery has bocce courts, a nice gift section, gracious grounds, and a stunning tasting room that looks through a glass wall at the barrels aging in their cellar. The tasting bar is nice and long. They produce widely respected Italian varietals, and they offer food pairings and library wines. They do great special events that are a lot of fun. One of the big benefits is their location, being just minutes from the Healdsburg plaza, you can include them in a tour of the downtown tasting rooms, or stop there on the way from one valley to another. The original family sold the winery but the new owners have happily changed very little. Map H

Selby Winery –Downtown Healdsburg – Tasting Room – Wines: Chardonnay, Sauvignon Blanc, Rosé, Syrah, Pinot Noir, Old Vine Zinfandel, Port, Merlot, Petite Syrah, Dolcetto, Semillon, Dessert – 215 Center St. Healdsburg CA 95448 – www.selbywinery.com – (707) 431-1288 – Hours: 11:00am –5:30pm – This is a small tasting room conveniently located across from the Oakville market and near the Healdsburg Plaza. Susie Selby is the winemaker and she sources her grapes from various areas around northern Sonoma. The tasting room is intimate, pretty and friendly and the wines are well made. Map H

Siduri Wines – Downtown Healdsburg – Wines: Pinot Noir – 235 Healdsburg Ave, Healdsburg, CA 95448 – www.siduri.com – (707) 578-3882 – Hours: 10:00am–4:30pm Friday – Sunday Appointment – The tasting room is in downtown Healdburg by the H2 Hotel. The wines are well regarded. Map H

Silver Oak Cellars – Alexander Valley – Big Reds – Wines: Cabernet Sauvignon Blend – 7300 Hwy 128 Healdsburg CA 95448 – www.silveroak.com – (707) 942-7082 – Hours: 9:00am–4:00pm – They produce an appealing Cabernet Sauvignon blend that they pour at both of their wineries; the other is in the Oakville section of the Napa Valley. There are distinct differences between the two areas; the Alexander Valley grapes produce softer and less tannic wines, the Napa wines are bigger and meaner. Just kidding! This is a state of the art winery and a gracious hospitality building on the Mayacamas benchlands. Map G

Simi Winery – Healdsburg – Great Tradition now in Corporate Ownership – Wines: Sauvignon Blanc, Chardonnay, Merlot, Cabernet Sauvignon – 16725 Healdsburg Ave. Healdsburg CA 95448 – www.simiwinery.com – (707) 433-6981 – Hours: 10:00am–5:00pm – Tours – This winery was founded in 1876 in San Francisco by two Italian brothers. In 1881, they moved the winery to Healdsburg. The daughter of one of the founders, Isabelle, ran the winery for many years and continued to make wine right through Prohibition, storing it in the cellars. While she had to sell many of their vineyards to survive, when Prohibition ended, she was one of the few companies with wine ready to sell. She sold the winery in 1970 and it has changed hands several times since then. They still make great wines; they have a friendly staff, and have both a gift and a picnic area. They are located just a few minutes from the Healdsburg Plaza. Map H

Simoncini Vineyards – Dry Creek Valley – Wines: Zinfandel Rose, Sauvignon Blanc – 2303 W. Dry Creek Road Healdsburg, CA 95448 – www.simoncinivineyards.com – (707) 433-8811 –

Hours: Seatings at 11:00am–2:00pm – Appointment – This is a charming family run winery on a stretch of the road with very few wineries, even though, as the crow flies, it is quite nearby. Their caves are cool and Dry Creek Valley is one of the prettiest areas in Northern California. Map F

Skip Stone Ranch – Collectors Alexander Valley – Wines: Oliver's Blend, Faultline Vineyard, Viognier, Rose, Malbec, Merlot 2505 Geysers Road Geyserville CA 95441 – (707) 433-9124 – Hours: Appointment – info@skipstoneranch.com – This is a tasting in the garden behind the home of the wealthy owner. The consulting winemaker is Phillipe Melka, who is known for making so many expensive Napa Cabs. From the seating area the views of the vineyards are great, although this area was hard hit in the 2019 fire that started a short distance away. Map G

Soda Rock Winery – Alexander Valley – Chardonnay, Sauvignon Blanc, Merlot, Primitivo, Zinfandel, Cabernet Franc, Cabernet Sauvignon, Malbec – 8015 Highway 128 Healdsburg, CA 95448 – www.sodarockwinery.com – (707) 433-3303 – Hours: 11:00am–5:00pm – This is owned by the Wilson family. The location has a long wine making tradition, but in the 2019 Alexander Valley fire most of the buildings on this site were destroyed. While they started to doing tastings fairly soon after, check with them on their current status. Map G

Sojourn Cellars – Downtown Sonoma – Tasting Room Changes Ahead – Wines: Cabernet Sauvignon, Pinot Noir – As of the beginning of 2021 they are located at 141 East Napa St. Sonoma CA 95476 – But, they are projected to move to their new winery location at 18701 Gehricke Rd. Sonoma CA – www.sojourncellars.com – (707) 933-9753 – Hours: 10:00am–5:00pm Appointment – They create good Pinot Noir and Cabernet Sauvignon. Why just those two wines? Because the two friends who started the winery like those two wines, so that is what they make. It is by appointment, for a seated tasting at a lovely conference table in the front room. The wines are elegant as is the experience. The current tasting room is just a short walk off the Plaza, down the street that was used for the filming of the movie Bottle Shock, about the Judgment of Paris. It beautifully portrayed a street in Paris with the help of a green screen. Map F

Sonoma Cutrer – Russian River Valley – Big Label with Croquet – Wines: Chardonnay, Pinot Noir – 4401 Slusser Rd Windsor CA – www.sonoma-cutrer.com – (707) 528-1181 – Hours: 10:00am–4:00pm This is a well-known label that is seen in many restaurants. It is a big estate and quite dramatic. The croquet courts were created by the original owner and are used for charity events. Map E

Spann Vineyards – Sonoma Valley Tasting Room – Wines: Cabernet Franc, Cabernet Sauvignon, Zinfandel, OMG, Petit Verdot, Zinfandel – 8910 Sonoma Highway, Kenwood CA – spannvineyards.com – (707) 707-282-9143 – Hours: 11:00am–6:00pm – Pizza and Wine Pairing – Chocolate & Wine Pairing. Map D

Spicy Vines Tasting Room – Downtown Healdsburg with Food Pairings – Wines: Pinot Noir, Chardonnay, Zinfandel, Cabernet Sauvignon – 441 Healdsburg Ave Healdsburg, CA 95448 – www.spicyvines.com – (707) 927-1065 – Hours: Check Website Appointment. Map H

Square Peg Winery – Russian River Valley – Dry Farmed Premium Pinot Noir by Allocation Outside Occidental – 4728 Stoetz Lane Sebastopol CA 95472 – www.squarepegwinery.com – (707) 827-1711 – Hours: 11:30am to 4:30pm.Map E

Starlite – Alexander Valley – Wines: Cabernet Sauvignon, Viognier, Zinfandel – 5511 Highway 128, Geyserville CA 95441 – www.starlitevineyards.com – (650) 464-7154 – Hours: 11:00am–5:00pm – Appointment – They sit alongside Highway 128 just north of Alexander Valley Road. They are nearby Jordan, Foley of Sonoma, Robert Young and Reeves. Map G

Stephen and Walker – Downtown Healdsburg – Tasting Room – Wines: Cabernet Sauvignon, Pinot Noir, Port, Zinfandel – 243 Healdsburg Ave. Healdsburg CA 95448 – www.trustwine.com – (707) 431-8749 – Hours: 11:00am–7:00pm – Their other name is the Trust Winery Limited. This is a simple tasting room just a few steps off the Plaza that sells the products of a wine making couple, hence, the two names. It is a long tasting bar, in a brightly lit room, with a collection of ceramics displayed for sale. The families that run it have been growing grapes and making wines in the area for years. Map H

Stonestreet Winery – Alexander Valley Grand Estate – Wines: Merlot, Cabernet Sauvignon, Chardonnay, Sauvignon Blanc – 7111 Highway 128 Healdsburg CA 95448 – www.stonestreetwinery.com – (707) 473-3333 – Hours: 10:00am–5:00pm varies with season – This winery sits about midway up the Alexander Valley, with the entrance just south of where Highway 128 turns and becomes Alexander Valley Road on the way to Healdsburg. It is a beautiful estate winery using hillside grapes. The views are pretty spectacular and from the winery, you can see the vineyards across the valley. This is a Jackson Family winery (of Kendall Jackson fame). They are across the way from Silver Oak Winery, and nearby are Robert Young and Foley of Sonoma. Map G

Stone Edge Farms – Sonoma Valley – Two Locations – Wines: Bordeaux Blends – 5700 Cavedale Rd, Glen Ellen, CA 95442 – (707) 935-6520 – Appointment – concierge@stoneedgefarm.com – The original location is at the south west edge of the Sonoma Valley, tucked up against the hills. The above location is at the upper edge of the Mayacamas Mountains along the Napa border on Cavedale Road. These are ultra-premium wines and both properties are sustainable. Map B

Stuhlmuller Vineyard – Alexander Valley – Wines: Cabernet Sauvignon, Zinfandel, Chardonnay – 4951 West Soda Rock Lane, Healdsburg, CA 95448 – www.stuhlmullervineyards.com

(707) 431-7745 Hours: Appointment Friday through Monday – This vineyard and winery sits on the western banks of the Russian River way down the road in Alexander Valley. It has great views of the valley and the wines are excellent. You can picnic on the patio. Map G

Suncé Winery – Russian River Valley – Wines: Chardonnay, Sauvignon Blanc, Pinot Noir, Zinfandel, Cabernet Sauvignon, Meritage, Barbera, Sangiovese, Cabernet Franc, Malbec, Syrah, Port, Petite Syrah – 1839 Olivet Rd. Santa Rosa CA 95401 – www.suncewinery.com – (707) 526-9463 – Hours: 10:30–5:00pm – Pronounced Soon–say! This is a cute tasting room. Considering how small and charming the place is, they produce an amazing variety of wines. They are one of the wonderful wineries on Olivet Road, including Hook and Ladder, DeLoach and Pellegrini. The staff is great, the tasting relaxed and they are convenient to numerous other wineries. Map E

Taft Street Winery – Russian River Valley – Sebastopol Casual – Wines: Merlot, Chardonnay, Pinot Noir, Sauvignon Blanc, Zinfandel, Syrah – 2030 Barlow Lane Sebastopol CA 95472 – www.taftstreetwinery.com – (707) 823-2049 – Hours: 11:00am–4:30pm Friday – Sunday – This is a funny little winery that sits off a bit by itself outside of the charming town of Sebastopol. It looks more like a wood yard than a winery, except for those big tanks, and the barrel racks. But do not be deceived, they make good wines, the tasting room is quite cute, and the staff is wonderful. We especially love the innovative way they have used old barrels for tasting tables, topping them with clear glass and tucking their numerous ribbons and medallions into the hollow below. They are near Balletto, Dutton Ranch and around the corner from the wonderful restaurant, Underwood Bar and Bistro in Graton. Map E

Talisman Wines – Glen Ellen Tasting Room – Wines: Pinot Noir – 13651 Arnold Dr, Glen Ellen, CA 95442 – www.talismanwine.com – (707) 721-1628 – Hours: 11-5 Appointment.

This charming tasting room sits in the little downtown Glen Ellen. The vineyards are in the southeast part of the valley where it is cool enough to grow good Pinot Noir. Map D

Talty Winery – Dry Creek Valley – Wines: Petite Syrah, Zinfandel – 7127 Dry Creek Road Healdsburg, CA 95448 – www.taltyvineyards.com – (707) 433-8438 – Hours: 12:00pm to 4:00pm – Appointment – Very much a small family grower and wine maker. Map F

Tara Bella Winery – Russian River Valley – Wines: Cabernet Sauvignon – 3701 Viking Road Santa Rosa, CA 95401 – www.tarabellawinery.com – (707) 544-9049 – Hours: Appointment – tarabellavines@gmail.com – This is a little jewel of a winery that quite surprisingly produces Cabernet, a heat loving grape, in the cool Russian River from their six acres of vines. Map E

The Spire Collection – Alexander Valley – Chardonnay, Sauvignon Blanc, Merlot, Primitivo, Zinfandel, Cabernet Franc, Cabernet Sauvignon, Malbec – 10075 Highway 128 Healdsburg, CA 95448 – www.membershipbyspire.com – (800) 544-7273 – Hours: 10:00am–3:30pm. This is a project on the site of the Fieldstone winery. Map G

Thomas George Estate – Russian River Valley – Hillside Caves – Wines: Chardonnay, Pinot Noir, Zinfandel, Viognier – 8075 Westside Road, Healdsburg CA 95448 – www.thomasgeorgeestates.com – (707) 431-8031 – Hours: 11:00am–5:00pm – They are located at the old Davis Bynum site that they have beautifully redone. They often taste in the cave. It sits on the hills above the Russian River and is reached by a steep driveway, leading up to a pretty clearing with picnic areas next to the tasting room. The vineyards in this area have always produced exceptional wines, so they are building on good foundations. This is an appealing and enjoyable experience. Map E

Three Sticks Wines – Downtown Sonoma Tasting Room – Wines: Pinot Blanc, Castenada Rose, Chardonnay – 143 W. Spain St, Sonoma, CA 95476 – www.threestickswines.com – (707) 996-3328 – Hours: 9:00am to 5:00pm – Appointment – The tasting of these premium wines takes place in a beautifully restored historic Adobe steps from the Sonoma Plaza. Map A

Thumbprint Cellars – Downtown Healdsburg Tasting Room – Wines: Bordeaux, Burgundy, Rhone, Zinfandel – 102 Matheson Street Healdsburg CA 95448 – www.thumbprintcellars.com – (707) 433-2393 – Hours: 11:00am–6:00pm – This is a long time, fun tasting room facing the Healdsburg plaza. They make good, moderately priced wines, and they have a fun staff. They have a wonderful, easy going style. Map F

Tin Barn Vineyards – Sonoma Valley – 8th Street Sonoma Winery Wines: Bordeaux, Burgundy, Rhone, Zinfandel – 21692 Eighth Street East, Suite 340 Sonoma, CA 95476 – www.TinBarnVineyards.com – (707) 938-5430 – Hours: 11:00am–4:00pm Saturday – Sunday – Weekdays Appointment – This is a small winery that produces good wines, located in a warehouse next to the Sonoma Airport. In that same complex are several small wineries, and some massive wine warehouses. Not surprisingly, the tasting is friendly and relaxed, it's hard to be overly formal when your front door is metal and the building is corrugated steel. The tasting room is high–ceilinged and spacious, and the interior windows look into the winery. Map B

Toad Hollow Vineyards – Downtown Healdsburg – Tasting Room – Wines: Bordeaux, Burgundy, Zinfandel – 409A Healdsburg Ave. CA 95448 – www.toadhollow.com – (707) 431-8997 – Hours: 10:00am–5:00pm – This is a cute tasting room just north of the Plaza with good wines and some neat gift items. They are a short walk to numerous other downtown tasting rooms and restaurants. The staff is fun and the tasting reasonable. Their vineyards are in the Russian River Valley. Map H

Trattore Farms Winery – Dry Creek Road – Wines: Burgundy, Bordeaux and Rhone plus Olive Oil & food pairings – 7878 Dry Creek Road Geyserville CA 95441 – www.trattorefarms.com – (707) 431-7200 – Hours: 11:00am–5:00pm Appointment. Grape vines and olive trees over forty rolling hillside acres. Trattore is Italian for tractor so obviously farming comes first here. Map F

Trentadue Winery –Alexander Valley – Italian Style – Wines: Sparkling, Zinfandel, Petite Syrah, Merlot, Cabernet Sauvignon, Viognier, Port, Old Patch Red. 19170 Geyserville Ave. Geyserville CA 95441 – www.trentadue.com – (707) 433-3104 – Hours: 10:00am–5:00pm This is an Italian American, family–owned and run winery with a long tradition that makes hospitality a way of life. They have created a beautiful property, well–made wines and a neat gift section. It feels like an Italian villa with gracious grounds and buildings suitable for events. Their original farm was in what is now Silicon Valley, and when the industry grew up around them, they moved to the Alexander Valley. Good choice! The name means 32 in Italian and the family comes originally from Bari on the Adriatic coast of Italy. They were part of thirty-two families that moved as a group. In 2019, the winery celebrated its 50th anniversary. Map G

Trione Vineyards – Alexander Valley – Hand Crafted – Wines: Bordeaux, Burgundy, Rhone Style Blend – 19550 Geyserville Avenue Geyserville, CA. 95441 – www.trionewinery.com – (707) 814-8100 – Hours: 10:00am–5:00pm Thursday – Sunday – This is a big winery just off of Highway 101, from a family with a long history in the Alexander Valley. It is located nearby Trentadue and the Frances Ford Coppola Winery. They make hand crafted wines from five estate vineyards in three Sonoma County appellations. Map G

Truett-Hurst Winery – Dry Creek Valley Charming – Wines: Zinfandel, Petite Syrah, Dessert – 5610 Dry Creek Rd. Healdsburg CA 95448 – www.truethurst.com – (707) 433-9545 –

Hours: 11:00am–5:00pm – This winery grows their grapes in a Biodynamic way, and their property includes diverse gardens, fruit trees, a beautiful patio, and a seating area along side the Dry Creek, which is not always dry. In fact, they often see trout swimming there. The tasting room is spacious and well lit, with two tasting bars. The staff is great, knowledgeable, engaged and fun. This is a partnership of three expert wine industry professionals and they've done a great job putting it together. This is also where the VML wines are being poured as of 2021. Map F

Twomey Healdsburg – Russian River Valley – Great Building with Views – Wines: Pinot Noir – 3000 Westside Rd. Healdsburg CA 95448 – www.twomeycellars.com – (800) 505-4850 – Hours: 11:00am–5:00pm – When they bought this winery from Roshambo it was already known for its dynamic architecture, and its great views of the valley in the distance. Twomey, which is part of the Silver Oak family, wanted a good site to make Pinot Noir, and the Russian River Valley is ideal for those grapes. The other Twomey winery is in Northern Napa and is known for their Merlot blends. Like most of the Silver Oak wineries, the staff here is friendly and relaxed, the gift shop is rather classic in selection, and the wines are well made, without a lot of flash, but with depth and integrity. Map E

Ty Caton Vineyards – Sonoma Valley – Tasting Room – Wines: Syrah, Bordeaux – 8910 Sonoma Highway. Kenwood CA 95452 – www.tycaton.com – (707) 833-0526 – Hours: 11:00am–5:00pm. Map D

Unti Vineyards – Dry Creek Valley – Respected Vineyard – Wines: Barbera, Syrah, Petite Syrah, Barbera Port – 4202 Dry Creek Rd. Healdsburg CA 95448 – www.untivineyards.com – (707) 433-5590 – Hours: 10:00am–4:00pm – This is a low keyed tasting in a newer space. The Unti Vineyard grapes are highly respected and sought after by winemakers, and their small winery produces wonderful wines. Map F

Valley of the Moon (Madrone) – Now Abbots Passage

Vérité – Alexander Valley Edge of Russian River Valley – 4611 Thomas Rd. Healdsburg CA 95448 – www.veritewines.com – (707) 431-3930 – Hours: 10:00am to 5:00pm Appointment – This is an ultra-premium winery owned by the Jackson Family, the owner of Kendall Jackson. They are located at the southern edge of the Alexander Valley nearby Lancaster, another ultra-premium producer. This area is where three American Viticulture Areas intersect, Alexander Valley, Knights Valley and Chalk Hill. Map E

Viansa Winery – Los Carneros on the Main Road – Italian Marketplace – Wines: Cabernet Sauvignon, Chardonnay, Barbera, Merlot, Nebbiolo Sangiovese, Dolcetto, Aleatico, Primitivo, Vernaccia, Pinot Grigio, Tocai, Cabernet Franc, Arneis,
Rosato – 25200 Arnold Dr. Sonoma CA 95476 – www.viansa.com – (707) 935-5738 – Hours: 10:00am–5:00pm. As you travel north on Highway 121 to Sonoma from San Francisco, after you pass the Raceway, you will see the terracotta colored roof of Viansa on a hillside to the right. It was started by Vicki and Sam Sebastiani, Vicki and Sam equals Vi–an–sa, although it is no longer owned by the Sebastiani family. It was designed in the style of an Italian villa. And comes complete with terraced vines, olive trees, tiles and of course, Italian grapes varietals like Vernaccia and Pinot Grigio. Their Pinot Grigio vines were some of the first to be planted in Carneros. They have a Deli/Market and picnic tables with wonderful views of Los Carneros and the bird sanctuary in the distance. The only downside of this lovely winery is that, thanks to its location, it is a favorite spot for bus groups coming from San Francisco conventions. Map B

Virginia Dare Winery - Now Called Francis Ford Coppola Too

Viszlay Vineyards – Russian River Valley – Wines: Cabernet Sauvignon, Syrah, Pinot Noir, Zinfandel – 851 Limerick Lane Healdsburg, CA 95448 – www.viszlayvineyards.com – (707) 481-1514 – Hours: 11:00am–5:00pm – Appointment. Map E

VJB Vineyards – Sonoma Valley – Tasting Room, Deli, Market and Espresso – Wines: Chardonnay, Cabernet Sauvignon, Syrah, Barbera, Super Tuscan – 9077 Sonoma Highway. Kenwood CA 95452 – www.vjbcellars.com – (707) 833-2300 – Hours: 10:00am–5:00pm – This may be the most welcoming winery in the Sonoma Valley because it contains not only a good tasting room with some stellar wines, but the Valley's best Italian deli and a beautiful Italian style courtyard filled with tables and a pizza kitchen. Of course, they also have an espresso bar and a wide range of interesting food items that they produce from their recipes. This is not surprising since the family is from Italy and they ran a successful restaurant in Santa Rosa for many years. Map D

VML - Sharing a Site with Truett Hurst Winery.

Wellington Vineyards – Sonoma Valley – Owned by the Belmonte Family that owns VJB – Great Old Vines – Wines: A new collection – 11600 Dunbar Rd. Glen Ellen CA 95442 – www.wellingtonvineyards.com – (707) 939-0708 – Hours: 11:00am–5:00pm – This quaint tasting room offers some unusual varietals that are all well–made from organic grapes. On the property are some beautiful old vines that go back to the prohibition era when growers shipped tons of grapes to home winemakers in the east. Since the Belmonte family purchased it they have been expanding and making improvements. Map D

Westerhold Family Vineyards – Santa Rosa – Wines: Pinot Noir, Chardonnay – 4949 Grange Road Santa Rosa, CA 95404 – (707) 586-9391 – Hours: Appointment – info@westerholdwines.com.

West Wines – Southern Dry Creek Valley – Wines: Cabernet Sauvignon, Sauvignon Blanc, Viognier, Blanc de Blanc 1000 Dry Creek Road Healdsburg, CA 95448 – (707) 433-2066 – Hours: 11:00am–5:00pm – Appointment. They are near the Wilson winery south of the Dry Creek Market. Map F

Westwood – Sonoma Plaza Tasting Room by Appointment – Wines: Pinot Noir, Syrah and Rhone blends – 11 E. Napa St. #3 Sonoma CA 95476 – www.westwoodwine.com – (707) 480-2251 – Hours: Appointment – This is a small winery with fantastic wines. If you are an enthusiast and collector seek them out because these wines are beautifully crafted. The tasting room is off the Sonoma Plaza down a long pathway, off a courtyard. Look for their small sign over head. The only glitch is that they are only by appointment. As of 2021 their wines are also being poured at Brasswood in Napa Valley. Map A

William Selyem – Russian River Valley – Wines: Zinfandel, Chardonnay, Pinot Noir, Gewurztraminer – 7227 Westside Road Healdsburg, CA 95448 – www.williamsselyem.com – (707) 433-6425 – tours@williamsselyem.com – This is a high-end producer in a remarkable building on Westside Road. They are very much by appointment and highly sought after. The grounds are interesting, with the buildings built around existing boulders. It is an unusual building for this region where most wineries tend towards ranch style or those that work in harmony with the land. This has a bit of an urban feel. Map E

Williamson Wines – Healdsburg Tasting Room with Pairings – Wines: Chardonnay, Pinot Noir, Merlot, Malbec, Shiraz, Cabernet Sauvignon – 134 Matheson Street Healdsburg CA 95448 – www.williamsonwines.com – (707) 473-0193 – Hours: 11:00am–7:00pm – These are some wonderful wines, and they take food pairing, designed to go with their wines, to a whole new level. They own and manage multiple vineyards, which may explain why they can offer such a wide variety of high–quality wines. Their home ranch is in the Dry Creek Valley, although the family is originally from Australia and they have that classic, relaxed hospitality. We have listed their first and current tasting room, located a few doors up Matheson Street from the Oakville Market, but they have several venues, as well as at their home ranch, which can be visited by appointment so check their website for current information. Map H

Wilson Winery – Dry Creek Valley Classic – Wines: Cabernet Sauvignon, Cabernet Franc, Zinfandel, Merlot, Syrah, Petite Syrah – 1960 Dry Creek Rd. Healdsburg CA 95448 – www.wilsonwinery.com – (707) 433-4355 – Hours: 11:00am–5:00pm – In terms of team spirit and winemaking skill, the Wilsons are stars. The outside of the building looks more like a barn than a winery, but do not be fooled, they produce some seriously good wines and pour them with style and enthusiasm. Folks leaves Wilson with a smile, and often a case or two of wine, as a result of good management, great teamwork and fun. The tasting room includes some nice gift items, wonderful views of the vineyards, and tables outside on the patio. The winery is one of the first places you come to on the left side as you travel up the valley from Healdsburg. The parking lot is just past the building. Look for the huge sculpture of a wolf in their front yard. Map F

Woodenhead Winery – Russian River Valley– Wines: Pinot Noir, Zinfandel – 5700 River Road, Santa Rosa 95401 – www.woodenheadwine.com – (707) 887-2703 – Hours: 10:30 to 4:30 Thursday – Monday – The entrance to this winery is just off River Road on the right as you head west. You reach the tasting room via a steep driveway, and then a series of stairs. The tasting room is intimate and friendly. The wines are good, the staff is knowledgeable and the owners may pour for you. They have some interesting items in their gift area, and the overall feeling in the tasting room is fun and social. They are near Martin Ray and Joseph Swan on the southern side of River Road. Map E

Yoakim Bridge Winery – Dry Creek Valley – Small and Charming Wines: Old Vine Zinfandel, Cabernet Sauvignon, Syrah, Merlot, Petit Syrah – 7209 Dry Creek Rd. Healdsburg CA 95448 – www.yoakimbridge.com – (707) 433-8511 – Hours: 11:00am–4:00pm Friday–Sunday Appointment – This is a charming Mom and Pop winery at the top of the Valley with beautiful old vines growing right outside the front door. The tasting room is small, so go with people you like. The people pouring for you are more than the likely the same people who made the wine, so if you have any questions they are happy to answer them. Navigation: They are located at the corner of Dry Creek Road and Yoakim Bridge Road. From here, you are just a few minutes from Ferrari–Carano, Sbragia, Zichichi, Preston and Bella. Map F

Zialena Winery – Alexander Valley – Wines: Cabernet Sauvignon, Zinfandel – 21112 River Road Geyserville CA 95441 – www.zialena.com – (707) 955-5992 – Hours: 10:00am – 4:30pm Appointment – Info@zialena.com – A family winery that has its history here for four generation, back to when the first member came from Carrara Italy to work in the Italian Swiss Colony winery. They have built a very modern winery and tasting room on their land in the northeast part of the valley nearby downtown Geyserville. Map G

Zichichi Vineyard and Winery – Dry Creek Valley – Wines: Zinfandel, Petite Syrah – 8626 W. Dry Creek Rd. Healdsburg CA 95448 – www.zichichifamilyvineyard.com – (707) 433-4410 – Hours: 11:00am–4:00pm – This is a small winery from a family that came here from New Orleans. They have a pretty tasting room with nice views of the northern valley. They often do both bar and barrel tastings. This is a nice treat since the barrel tasting lets people see how the wines develop during their process. They have a nice team and they make some interesting wines. Navigation: They are located at the corner of West Dry Creek Road and Yoakim Bridge Road. From here, you are near Yoakim Bridge, Ferrari Carano and Sbragia. Map F

Zina Hyde Cunningham Winery – Tasting Room on the Sonoma Plaza inside the Ledson Hotel– Wines: Sauvignon Blanc, Chardonnay, Pinot Noir, Carignane, Zinfandel – www.zinawinery.com – (707) 895-9462 – The roots of this winery go back to the mid-1800's in Sonoma and Mendocino and it is associated with the Ledson Winery. Map A

ZO Wines – Dry Creek Valley– Wines: Zinfandel, Sauvignon Blanc, Chardonnay, Viognier, Pinot Noir – 3232 Dry Creek Road Healdsburg CA 95448 – www.zowines.com – (707) 794-6060 – Hours: 11:00am–5:00pm – Appointment – info@zowines.com – A small family winery at the south end of Dry Creek Road just north of Healdsburg. Map F

Zouzounis Wines (Previously Deux Amis) – Windsor Corporate Park – Pinot Noir, Cabernet Sauvignon, Petite Syrah and a Port, Zinfandels – 7680 Bell Road, Windsor (Windsor Beverage District) – www.zouzouniswines.com – (707) 431-7945 – Hours: 1:00pm – 5:00pm Saturday to Sunday Appointment.

Sonoma Valley with the Towns of Wine Country

About the Authors

Ralph and Lahni DeAmicis backed into writing tour and travel books by starting to create a book about winery buildings for their series on Feng Shui, but the research was going excruciatingly slow. While the winery staff knew the wines, they rarely knew about the buildings. Then one day, while coming out of the Stag's Leap Wine Cellars, Ralph chatted up a local limousine driver who was a wealth of information about interesting winery buildings, apparently that knowledge was part of a tour guide's toolbox.

Seeing a research opportunity that would also put some money in their pockets, Ralph got a part time job driving tours, coming home daily with notes and photographs of the wineries. As he navigated his way around the various valleys, they realized that even though the wineries are the biggest attraction, there wasn't a good 'winery' tour book. So, their project about buildings morphed into their first guide book in 2008, becoming the first in a series of updates and improvements.

After two years of touring for other companies Ralph & Lahni decided to start their own tour company, Amicis Tours, to make the continuing research easier. They soon realized that it's a fun business that brings them to beautiful places while connecting them to the winemaking community. In 2012 they started producing the TV show 'Wine Country at Work' which allowed them to more deeply explore topics that they found interesting. In 2021 they are publishing their first travel book, 'Wine Country in Shorts', which are the stories about the area that they have been telling to clients over their shoulders for years. A couple of bonus chapters from that book are included here for your enjoyment! But, before that is an extra bonus chapter on visiting Wine Country with children. Find their books and videos at:

www.WineCountryAtWork.com

Next, a Bonus Chapter

Visiting with Children

WARNING: The most important thing to remember when you come to Wine Country with children is that this is a place where people drink alcohol, and you need to plan on having a disciplined, designated driver the entire time. Napa and Sonoma have twice the DUI rate of the rest of California, and the only reason they do not have more is because they have a limited police budget. DUI's in California are very expensive, but when a person gets caught driving under the influence with a child on board, that adds a charge of 'child endangerment' to the list. As if that were not enough to make people act like good parents, remember this, when you are driving along these narrow country roads, you are sharing them with a shockingly high number of drunk drivers. So, not only do you need to guard against your own excesses, but you need to be continually on guard against theirs. It is much easier for a sober driver to do that successfully!

Sonoma and the Valley of the Moon

The Northern California Wine Country has often been described as a 'Disneyland for Adults', but that doesn't mean you have to leave the children behind. For many people, visiting wineries is only one day of their trip to San Francisco and with all the attractions it has to offer, the Bay Area is a great destination for the whole family. A daytrip to the scenic counties of Sonoma and Napa provides an opportunity to enjoy a relaxed pace with stunning views, wonderful tours, interesting wineries and of course wine.

The wineries and their gift shops are admittedly more interesting to the adults than the kids, but they can still enjoy the trip because it is, after all, farm country, and what kid doesn't enjoy that? Sonoma especially takes great pride in their agricultural diversity, so as you travel around you're going to see a wide variety of plantings, orchards and livestock in between the vineyards. Of the various counties, we have to say that larger and more convenient Sonoma, with its scenic ocean coastline and redwood forests, is more conducive to visiting with children.

The secret to having a great time together is to realize that while many wineries are not suitable or enjoyable for children, there are some that handle them better. Sonoma and Napa have hundreds of wineries that can be visited easily, but maybe one percent of them can accommodate children well. Luckily, Sonoma has other family-friendly attractions.

The most kid friendly and parent enjoyable destination is the Plaza in downtown Sonoma. This is the 'Philadelphia of California', because it is the place where the Republic of California declared its independence from Mexico. If you're coming from San Francisco over the Golden Gate Bridge you'll be at this historic and charming place in about forty-five minutes. As you are driving up Broadway towards the Plaza you are pointed due north, so to the right is east (Napa County) and to the left is west (The Town of Petaluma).

Here is another helpful navigation tip, realize that there are the two counties, Sonoma and Napa, there are the two cities, Sonoma and Napa. While Napa is a city of about eighty thousand people, Sonoma is small, with only about ten thousand people, but it is big in history. Sonoma is the only city in California that enjoys all three of these distinctions; it was an official Pueblo, or city under Mexico, it was a Franciscan Mission (the twenty-first and final), and it was the military headquarters for Northern California under both Mexico and the United States.

Placed around the Plaza, which is the largest in California, are numerous museums that you can visit with children, including the San Francisco Solano Mission, with their original olive trees and the soldier's Barracks. When you pay for these two sites, it includes a visit to the Vallejo Homestead, a short drive to the west on Spain Street, amidst a large park. This was the home of General Mariano Guadalupe Vallejo, Napa's most prominent citizen and quite a colorful character. On the north side of the plaza is a sculpture of him sitting on a bench, which was very suitable, because he was a beloved figure. At the northeast corner of the plaza is the monument for the raising of the Bear Flag in 1846, when California independence was declared. Just a few steps away are two excellent playgrounds, geared to younger and older children. All around the perimeter of the plaza are restaurants, shops and a multitude of excellent tasting rooms, so there is something for everybody.

The Plaza is home to a wonderful collection of mature trees, so the picnic tables near the playgrounds and the popular duck pond in the southwest corner are nicely shaded in the warm weather. On the eastern edge of the Plaza is the tourist bureau which is filled with helpful information about the Valley of the Moon, as Sonoma is known. It is located in an old Carnegie Library building and it can provide additional information for a great day with kids. A unique attraction for younger children is Train Town, located just five minutes south of the Plaza on Broadway. This old-style amusement park is on the register of historic places. Built in the 1920's, there is a small train ride and a traditional merry-go-round and it harkens back to a time before special effects were digital. There is even a petting zoo.

In recent years the number of tasting rooms around the Plaza dramatically escalated and you can taste some excellent wines there, without spending the whole day driving. In between you can visit the playground and the ice cream shop to keep the kids happy. Five minutes east of the Plaza is a Sonoma original, the Sebastiani Family Winery, with their great old barrel room which will amaze the children. A little further east is California's most historic winery, Buena Vista. While we can't say that they cater to children, older kids will appreciate the educational programs, the history and the architecture. They do great walking tours with hosts in period costumes and the pathway down to the winery features a wonderful historical timeline done in full size figures perched against the hillside.

Just to the south of town is the family friendly Larson Winery, on the old Sonoma Rodeo site. This was where the champion racehorse Sea Biscuit stabled overnight when he was racing on the West Coast. It has a farm-like setting with llamas and sheep. Horse rides through the vineyards can often be arranged in advance, bocce courts and picnic areas round out the experience.

From the Plaza you can head north on Highway 12 up the lovely Valley of the Moon to Glen Ellen. Just up the hill from the little downtown you will find a winery that has Sonoma's best tours, the Benziger Family. Their experiences offer a wonderful mix of agriculture, education and fine wine. Their vineyards are tucked in a pretty little valley on Sonoma Mountain just down the hill from Jack London's old "Beauty Ranch", now a park. Their main tour is aboard a tram attached to the back of a tractor, and it winds its way up into the vineyards where they explain the biodynamic approach to agriculture. This is a remarkable system that is increasingly popular with many high-end wineries. Next you visit the barrel caves and finish up in the winery for a tasting. Admittedly wineries are about adult enjoyment, but there are often older children on the Benziger tour and they always seem to enjoy themselves, after all, it's pulled by a tractor.

Please don't make the mistake of bringing children to trendy wineries where they have nothing of interest for kids, because it annoys everybody else there. Also, don't expect kids to be happy in the tasting room, for them the hour while you are tasting wine is boring. The wineries that are kid friendly have made a big effort to be so. At both the Sonoma Plaza and Benziger you'll find good picnic tables, so pick up some sandwiches at one of the downtown markets. This is more enjoyable and less stressful than bringing children to a busy restaurant. You can even order a pizza at Mary's on the Plaza and enjoy it at a picnic table, which goes great with Zinfandel. This is important to know because, unlike most parks, you can drink wine on the Sonoma Plaza and there are plenty of places to buy a bottle.

Several of the wineries in the Valley of the Moon are kid friendly as long as you have an adult willing to keep an eye on them. Some of the grounds are gracious and park-like allowing for a little outdoor enjoyment in beautiful surroundings, including Imagery, Landmark, Saint Francis, Chateau Saint Jean and the Ledson Winery. Those final two both have small deli markets and picnic tables on site. Although, the best place for lunch with a family is the VJB winery and market. This Italian style property has a large central seating area, and it is possible to arrange, in advance, for your tasting to accompany your lunch. They have wonderful food and of course a pizza oven. All these wineries are within five miles of each other along Highway 12, the main road in the Valley. Hint: Bring a soccer ball or a Frisbee. There are some great lawns in the Valley of the Moon, and folks in Sonoma are generally more relaxed and casual than those in Napa.

Over the years wineries have increasingly moved away from tasting bars to seated experiences. This is actually a benefit for those traveling with a child, but check with the staff when you make your reservation, so that they can place your group in a suitable area, out of the flow of traffic. Realize that while the staff will be polite enough, they will be concerned about whether the presence of children in an environment not designed for them, will affect the other guest's enjoyment. Tasting fees can be quite expensive, and they have a narrow window each day for sales. It was well-known among tasting room managers that cute kids, babies and dogs at a tasting can do horrible things to their sales numbers, by distracting the guests so they don't give their full attention to the wine.

The wineries of northern Sonoma are amazingly un-kid friendly, because they are generally smaller, and have shorter operating hours. That doesn't mean that they don't like children, this is farm country after all, and that means families matter. It's just that these are little places that operate on tight margins and kids don't fit into their equation. The very big exception to this is the Francis Ford Coppola winery in Geyserville. This was designed as a destination, and it includes two restaurants, a swimming pool and a movie museum. Downtown Healdsburg has a bit of the feel of downtown Sonoma, with a smaller, but charming central plaza. So it's a nice place to stroll with children and it is home to a wealth of tasting rooms, although it lacks the Sonoma Plaza's expansive playgrounds.

Visiting Napa with Children

Napa is a great place for adults to visit because the wineries are close together, making it easy to visit the ones you want to in a day trip. Because half of the vineyards grow Cabernet Sauvignon, one of the most expensive grapes, Napa's wines are generally are more expensive than Sonoma's. The whole valley is only thirty miles long by five miles wide and the selection of wineries that are easy to reach is wonderful.

However, being only one third the size of Sonoma, Napa is not agriculturally diverse, growing wine grapes and the making the finished product are their main occupation, tourism is a sideline. Napa is another half hour farther from the Golden Gate Bridge, but the ride brings you through the beautiful Los Carneros district with its vineyard covered hills that have a distinctly Tuscan feeling. Napa is closer to San Francisco via the less scenic, but often more trafficked Bay Bridge.

Downtown Napa has more of a city style than its Spanish influenced cousin Sonoma, but up in the valley there are few places that very young children will enjoy or feel welcome. However, for older children and even teenagers, there are some good attractions, because almost everyone enjoys spectacular architecture and great views, things at which Napa excels. A classic example of this is the Artesa Winery, with its hilltop site overlooking Los Carneros and the Bay. But in 2021 Artesa, like many other wineries, made it policy to not admit children or dogs.

Just to the north in Yountville is Domaine Chandon, one of Napa's original makers of sparkling wine. This is a favorite for groups and people with children because the grounds are gracious and accommodating, with lawns, ponds and wildlife. Up on the patio, they offer snacks along with their elegant sparkling wines and the tables make it easier to keep everyone together. The springtime tadpole explosion in the ponds will keep any child entertained.

One of the most enjoyable family wineries is Inglenook in Rutherford, about halfway up the Napa Valley on Highway 29 (St. Helena Highway). It is owned by Francis Ford and Elenore Coppola. In 2021 they sold their other two California wineries. They took Napa's historic Neibaum/Inglenook building and surrounded it with gardens that have all of the graciousness of a southern Italian villa. The exhibits and old barrel rooms upstairs are enough to entertain most children. During the summer they provide model sailboats to send gliding on the fountain pool in front of the building. There is a small café, with outdoor seating and some food. They also have a very grown-up gift shop and of course some wonderful wines for the adults. With a child, rather than booking a tasting, make an appointment for a Bistro seating where you can sit outside and choose wines by the glass and the children can be outside on those beautiful grounds.

Just to the north of Inglenook across from a large market is the V. Sattui Winery, which in this context is most valuable for their great deli offerings and large picnic area. Napa does not have a lot of picnic areas, and this is one of the only deli markets in a winery. On weekends V. Sattui gets crazy busy, but finding food, wine and picnic tables all together certainly makes the logistics of blending wineries with children much easier. The wineries have about twenty-five to thirty percent more traffic on Saturdays than Sundays, and of course touring during the week with kids offers a lot of advantages. Because of the lack of picnic tables it is important to plan your day around your lunch, and with kids plan to eat early to avoid the rush.

Kids in the Wilds of Calistoga

For the San Francisco-based traveler, if you are up for a ride, two of the most interesting wineries for children are in the northern part of the Napa Valley, just south of the 'old west' style town of Calistoga. This is a great, kid-friendly town to visit onto itself. These two wineries are not suitable for infants in strollers, but for children eight years and older they are a fun experience. First is Sterling Vineyards, famous for its aerial tramway that carries visitors to its hilltop winery. Many years ago it was one of the first large wineries to charge for their tastings. The price includes the tram ride. Between the tram, the gift shop and the tasting you need to allow an hour and a half to two hours to enjoy the place. Get there early to avoid the lines. While it is far from ideal for children, it is different from the standard tasting experience. The 2020 fires burned all around the winery and getting it up and running again will take time. As of August 2021 it was still closed.

Across Highway 29 and a bit to the south is the Castello di Amorosa, which was built to look like an authentic Tuscan castle, from real stone and hand wrought iron. Children are restricted to the early morning tours so you should check their website for the schedule. The tour with tasting takes about two hours. The fees for Napa wineries are all in the higher range, although there may be some discounts for children. Napa gets hot in the summer, but very dry, so there are very few flying bugs. During the winter it gets rainy, but not very cold. Both Spring and Fall are gorgeous, and harvest time, from late August through mid-November is a very busy and exciting time in Wine Country.

Finally, small, private wineries are often at people's homes, so for the collector, traveling with children, you should ask your potential hosts if children are welcomed. If you want to get to the smaller wineries, ask your hotel to arrange a babysitter. Touring with children can be educational and a lot of fun, if you visit wineries that they'll find interesting too. So, choose well and enjoy your day with the kids in Wine Country.

Two Bonus Chapters from 'Wine Country in Shorts'
A Tale of The Russian River Valley

Names are different from words, in the way that we accept them. We think of words as part of a sentence communicating an idea, like interdependent planets in their own Solar System, spinning around the Sunny subject and Lunar object. But names are like comets and islands, practically sovereign nations accepted at face value, with all their complicated history. Consider the name Chardonnay, a popular white wine grape that appears on many menus. People rarely wonder about that name's origin or meaning. They assume it's French, since the most famous representatives are from Burgundy and Champagne. Maybe the name means something in a local Patois and thus, like so much about the French countryside, its history is obscure and complicated. But Chardonnay's name instead traces back to the Middle East, Syria, Lebanon and Israel where the grape was discovered by the Crusaders. Chardonnay means the Gates of God in those languages, which says much about the importance they ascribed to that pretty, luminous grape and its tremendously adaptable wine.

Coincidentally, Chardonnay is one of the two most popular grapes grown in the North Bay region whose names also have complicated and exotic histories. One of those is the Russian River Valley. People rarely ask us about the source of that name, yet we've lost count of the number of clients who were surprised that the Russians had settled in that green expanse north of San Francisco. Why else would they call that shallow, winding river, that carries the silt and scent of the mountains all the way the Pacific the 'Russian' River? People just accept names without thinking, like New Yorkers accept the Russian Tearoom Uptown and the Russian Baths downtown, even though both are far from Moscow and longtime Manhattan institutions.

Why would the Russians come to Northern California? Well first of all, why wouldn't they. Russia sailors have way too much experience with ice, whether it is navigating the Baltic Sea, or the Pacific coast north of Vladivostok. That northern seaside city sits at the tip of the broad Siberian plateau, a place that Americans view as a great wasteland, but it is an area of huge resources. Wherever there are things to sell and deep-water ports, there is the potential for commerce and Vladistock is Russia's gate way to the Pacific rim and America's west coast.

It is easy to forget now that Russia once controlled Alaska which it sold to the United States in the 1800s for sizable payment. At the time of the sale, it was called Seward's folly, for the Secretary of State who negotiated the sale. Considering the gold and oil Alaska contains, that turned out to be a good deal. For the Russians, exploiting Alaska was difficult because of the great distances and harsh weather. While the fur trade was very profitable, sustaining the colony was a Labor of Hercules, because transporting food from Russia to Alaska over the Trans-Siberian railway was an exercise in futility.

If the food wasn't stolen by officials or brigands along the way, it likely rotted during the long rail trip and ensuing sea voyage. To feed their people it was decided to look in a different direction, and the most practical direction was south along the Pacific coastline and warmer weather. A ship was dispatched to find a good location for their settlement.

As the Russians sailed south, they knew that the land they were planning on settling had been claimed by Sir Walter Raleigh, when he landed north of San Francisco in the late 1600s in his ship the Golden Hind. But he did not linger there, because he was focused on circumnavigating the globe.

Poor sir Walter, he should have recognized a good thing when he found it. Because he missed discovering the inlet that today is called the Golden Gate, the pathway to one of the world's greatest harbors, by about 10 miles. It was exactly that kind of ideal port, protected from the weather and fed by many navigable rivers, that explorers searched the globe for. Admittedly, the Golden Gate is hard to find from the ocean side, but he was so close, but no cigar. Instead, he landed on the wet, marshy, foggy shores of Point Reyes and the rain swept hills of Bodega Bay, before setting out across the Pacific. He probably encountered the outlet of the Russian River, but that was too shallow and shoal clogged to navigate with a sailing ship.

They also knew that the Spanish claimed all the land in California south of San Francisco, and a bit to the north, but their military might was sorely lacking in the neighborhood, so it would be hard for them resist a little settlement. Ignoring both the English and Spanish claims, the Russians found a likely spot along the California Coast in Sonoma, seventy miles north of the Spanish settlements in San Francisco. Unlike Sir Walter, they were accustomed to wet and cool places, and the Sonoma Coast was a nice change from the frozen north. While there is plenty of sunshine during the day, the nightly fog keeps the hillsides green for much of the year, making it an ideal place for raising food and grazing their livestock.

It didn't take them long for them to realize how well they had chosen. The region is such a garden of Eden that the famous botanist Luther Burbank, who developed many of our popular fruit varieties, said that of all the places on earth this was the area most blessed by nature. Everything grows well there, from palm trees to apples, from grapes to redwoods. Admittedly, Luther had his farm about forty miles east from the cooler Russian settlements, on the softly rolling plains between the Sonoma Valley and the Russian River Valley.

While the Russians were grateful for the warm weather and easy growing conditions, they did suffer from having rowdy neighbors, the Spanish, the Americans and the Pomo Tribes.

If they had explored earlier, they could have sailed through the Golden Gate and claimed that marvelous port before the Spanish. But the Spanish Galleons had been sailing these shores for more than a hundred years before the Russians, first sailing into the San Francisco Bay in 1775. The Spanish outpost there was small, because that was the northern tip of their holdings in the Americas. They had an advantage over the Russians because they were connected by land to their military outpost in Monterey, by El Camino Real, or the 'Royal Road'. This path ran north from Guatemala through Mexico City, on through the American southwest and up the Pacific coast, linking the Franciscan Missions together.

Being careful to not intrude on their Spanish neighbors to the south, the Russians established their Fort Ross north of the Russian River. While it was built like a fort with four strong walls and cannons, it was not manned by soldiers, but by traders, trappers and administrators. The Russians brought Aleut Indians from Kodiak Island in Alaska to hunt the seals and sea otters. The sea otter pelts were some of the valuable in the world, and there was a good market for them among the Chinese aristocracy. Supposedly, the Emperor wore clothes trimmed with California sea otter fur. While the men and their kayaks traveled along the coast in sailing ships, the women farmed the land, producing the foods that were shipped north.

Just because the traders and trappers were not soldiers didn't stop them from firing the canons when they had too much to drink, which was apparently a daily occurrence. It happened so much that the bookkeeper for the settlement complained about the expense for gun power.

Which brings us once again to names, Fort Ross. Who was this guy named Ross? Here we see an example of 'Californeese', a dialect similar to Spanglish, where words from different languages are married together. The English word 'Fort' is married to 'Ross', which comes from the Russian word 'Rossiya', which means 'Mother Russia'. The Russians, which included a variety of Eastern Europeans, such as the Bohemian (Polish) brothers who established the Korbel winery, were well liked in the area. They were considered very honest in their trading and easy to work with, compared to the imperious Spanish, who felt justified enslaving the native people.

In a land where most of the westerners were from other places, the Russians were a pleasant contribution. Culturally they were reigned over by the very beautiful and refined Princess Ilona de Gargorin. This young woman was married to the Count who was the manager at the Fort Ross. But that's another story!

The Sonoma Mission, San Francisco Solano, was established in the 1820's, in concert with a military base or Presidio, commanded by General Vallejo, as a way to prevent the Russians from spreading their trading market south into the marginal Spanish territory. But always the good host, General Vallejo invited the Count and the Princess to his home for a feast. Then he had to convince his friend and ally, Chief Solano, a towering, charismatic brave, to not kidnap the beautiful Ilona.

Russia held onto their Fort until it became clear that California was going to permanently become part of the United States, at which point they sold it to John Sutter, of gold rush fame, who never paid that bill. Why did they give up such a prime location? Because they were afraid of their people becoming infected with democracy!

But even though the Russians left their Fort Rossiya, there are still many local families that trace their roots back to that Sonoma Coast settlement, where the frozen Alaskans just wanted a warm place to raise their food and their children.

Another Bonus Chapter
A Tale of Napa's Silverado Trail

The Silverado Trail is the quintessential California road that travels along the eastern side of the Napa Valley, at the foot of the Vaca mountains. It started as a native trail that wound its way up into the hills to get above the winter flooding on the valley floor. It was made into a road by the western settlers in the 1860s to provide a winter alternative when the main road, Saint Helena Highway, washed out in the winter rains. Before that the trail served an important role in the tribal economies. The original, one-person wide path stretched from the southern foot of Mount Saint Helena, for a two day walk south along the eastern hills, to the meeting of the valley's central river, and a large creek. At that spot, the river gets dramatically deeper and straighter. From there the natives could take their reed boats, or sákas, for a smooth paddle of a few hours, south to the bay. There they would meet with the tribe of 'traders', or 'Carquinez', whose village sat at the narrows where the Napa River meets the larger Sacramento River, as they empty into the great bay. But what were the Napa tribes trading?

There were several tribes in the Napa Valley, but the upper part had been taken over by the warlike Onosai, the 'Outspoken Ones', that the Spanish called Wappo, for brave. By spreading south from the lake country, they gained control of the black volcanic glass deposits at the northern part of the trail. This 'obsidian' was formed millions of years ago when silica rich lava plunged into cold water, producing a fractured glass that is both strong and incredibly sharp. The Onosai depended on the trail and the river to trade their knives, arrowheads, hatchets, and scraping tools, with the Carquinez, who in turn traded them throughout the bay area. The tribes called that vital convergence of the waters where the river deepened, the 'fairy village', or 'Napa'. It was so important to the valley's wellbeing that it was open to all without conflict. Admittedly, no tribe was inclined to establish a large camp there, because it suffered from the valley's worst floods. Today that meeting of the rivers is in downtown Napa and until the river was 'fixed' in 2005, shopkeepers always kept sandbags handy waiting for the next deluge!

Not surprisingly, the settlers also valued that meeting of the waters for the same reason. The fertility and abundance of the valley attracted sailing ships, looking for produce to trade, and that meeting of the waters in downtown Napa is the farthest northern point on the river where a sailing ship can navigate year-round. Some of the valley's earliest investors were sea captains, who saw the possibilities and settled there. Several of the valley's most historic wineries were built in the 1800's by partners in a shipping company that had made fortunes transporting goods during the Alaska gold rush. There are two stories behind the trail's distinctive name. The first starts with the gold rush in the Sierra Madre mountains, a five-day wagon ride to the east, in good weather. It attracted so many hopeful prospectors from around the world, that sailing ships arriving in San Francisco's harbor were often stranded there when the crews abandoned them and headed for the hills. But refining gold requires mercury to capture the grains mixed with the sand, so when that liquid metal was discovered on Mount Saint Helena, at the top of the valley, that became a new opportunity for the miners.

'Helena', as she is known locally, is just 5000 feet tall. She's a pretty mountain with an elegant volcanic cone, that every five years or so sees a frosting of snow. When she erupted three million years ago, along with her sisters, Mounts Sonoma and Hood, they shaped this area's distinctive look. The mercury miners, who were a particularly loony lot, due to their exposure to that metallic neuro toxin, named the trail after mercury's contemporary title, Quicksilver. So the Silverado Trail was named for the Roman God who is the patron of healers and writers, it is intriguing how that later played out. Then silver was discovered on the mountain and those miners assumed that the name 'Silverado Trail' related to that metal, and that is usually the story that you will hear! This theme of stories having multiple versions is common in Wine Country, for instance, three different people claim to have named Mount Saint Helena.

As the wagon traffic up valley expanded the locals made the trail into a road. Gradually its path moved to the west, closer to the edge of the valley floor, but there are still parts that overlay the original, single person wide path, where countless feet carried food, supplies and obsidian tools. The 'Trail' was never as well-known as Saint Helena Highway, because that travels through the wide, flat valley floor, with its rich, deep soils. The Silverado Trail instead skirts the rocky, steep benchlands formed by the volcanic ridges that line the eastern edge of the valley. When the railroad tracks were laid to bring tourists to Calistoga's healing hot springs, they were run alongside the main road. So, while the Trail was locally helpful, it was relatively unknown, until some small fame came to it thanks to a Scottish author.

Robert Louis Stevenson was very much in love with Fanny Van de Grift, an American magazine writer he met in Europe. But, despite his malnourished, pale appearance, love of drink and uncertain income, she resisted his proposal for marriage. She left him, and England's wet climate and booked passage on a sailing ship to California, at a time when the ships traveled around the treacherous tip of South America. She arrived safe, but sickly from the arduous journey. But Stevenson was a poet in love, so he followed her, arriving in San Francisco in an equally pitiful state, with no guarantee that Fanny had not, in the interim, found herself a new, tall, strong and tan lover, as we imagine all Californians to be. Fortunately for RLS, Fanny had not replaced him in her heart, and opened her loving arms to his renewed marriage proposal. After all, he had just left everything behind, crossed oceans and traveled practically halfway around the world to find her, so he was obviously committed!

They married in San Francisco and their friends suggested that the skinny, sickly newlyweds honeymoon at the healing spas of Napa. They had become famous for their ability to restore health. They initially stayed at the Hotel Saint Helena, and found the climate kind, the air and food wonderful and the sunlight spectacularly luminous. So, they searched for a way to extend their stay that would not use up their limited funds. Some locals pointed the young couple towards an abandoned mining camp on the flanks of Mount Saint Helena, where they found a two-story cabin to squat in, for an extended honeymoon. As they gradually regained their vitality in this new Eden, Robert and Fanny were impressed by the beauty of the place. Not surprisingly their appreciation found its way into his writings.

In his most famous book 'Treasure Island', 'Lookout Mountain' was based on Mount Saint Helena, where they made their first home together, and there was more! During their sojourn they traveled throughout the valley, including to the nearby Schramsberg winery. They were thoroughly impressed by the wonderful location, the beautiful buildings, the barrel caves dug by Chinese miners and their generous host's excellent wines. Robert and Fanny must have been amazed by the Schram's success. Here was Jacob, a German immigrant barber, married to Annie, a local girl, who together farmstead a heavily wooded, up valley hillside that they turned it into their paradise.

This story was contained in a travel log that Stevenson wrote called the 'Silverado Squatters'. It contains the often-quoted phrase, for which Napa marketing folks have been eternally grateful, "and their wines were bottled poetry". But how did these young folks, without much money, get around the valley in the 1880's? At that time people either walked, rented horses or a wagon, or depended on the flexibility and generosity of the local stagecoach drivers, who plied the Saint Helena Highway and the Silverado Trail! The coach line that ran along the Silverado was driven by a very tall, colorful gent called 'Long' John. He was known locally as John Silverado, after his popular route. As any reader of the great adventure novel 'Treasure Island' knows, the swashbuckling, peg-legged pirate at the heart of that story is named Long John Silver! I have often wondered if that flamboyant wagon master, a predecessor of the local tour guides, who are themselves a colorful group, happened to wear a patch over one eye? Argh!

The Sonoma Plaza

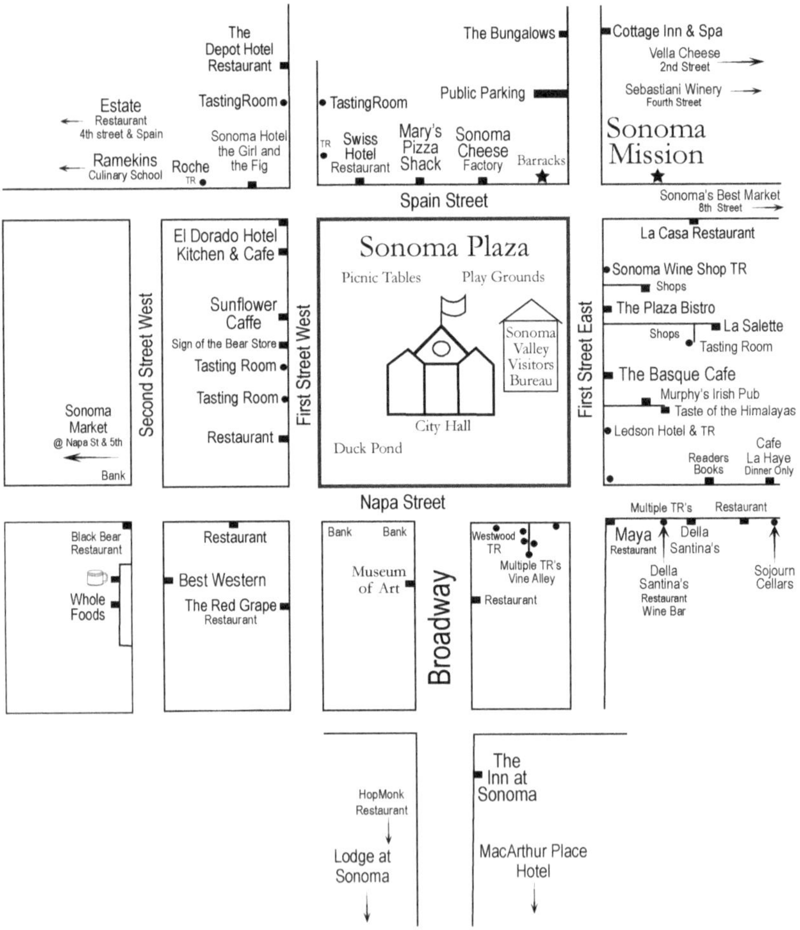

First Stops Coming from the South

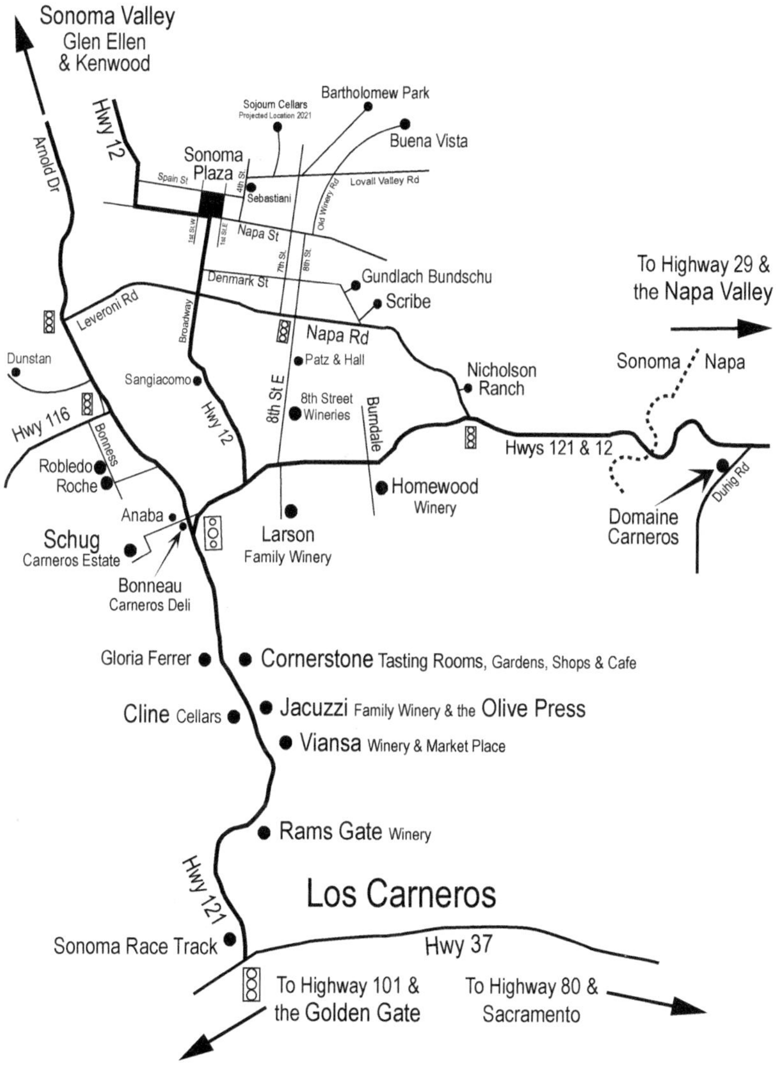

Los Carneros AVA

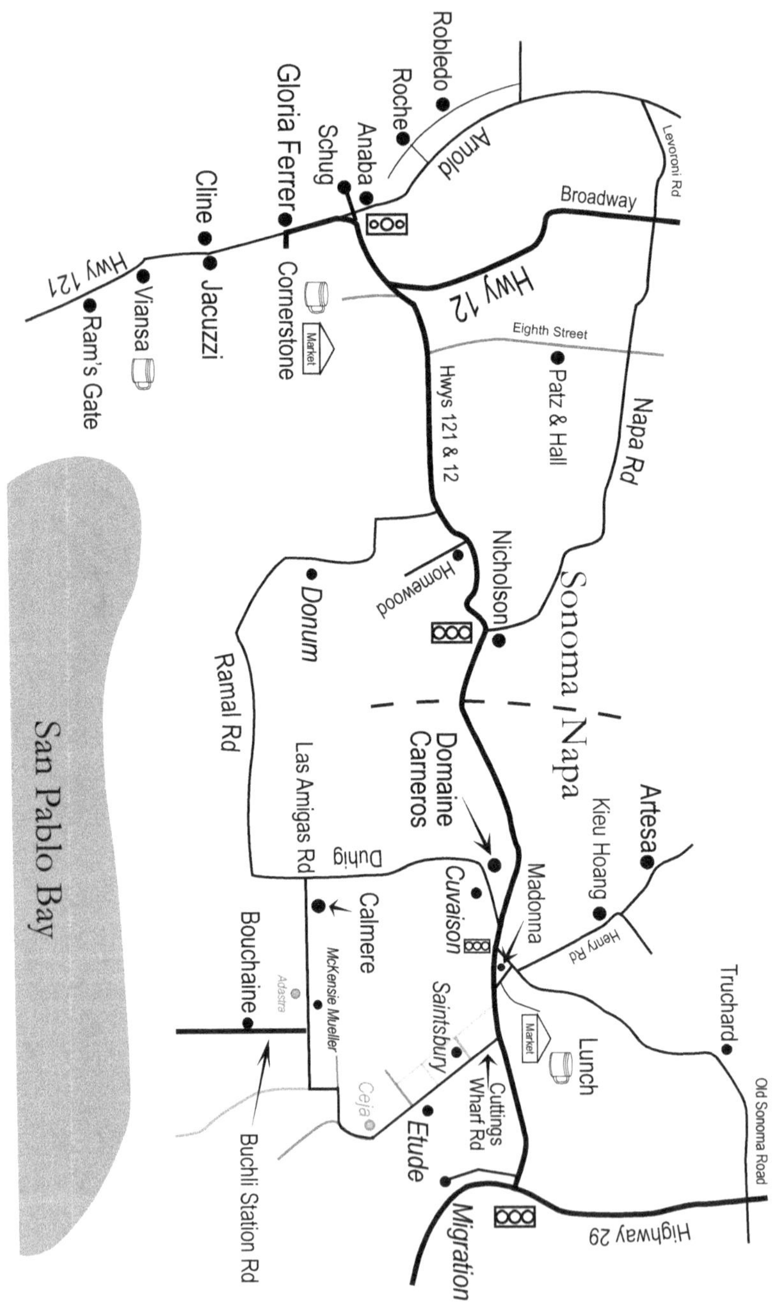

Sonoma Valley

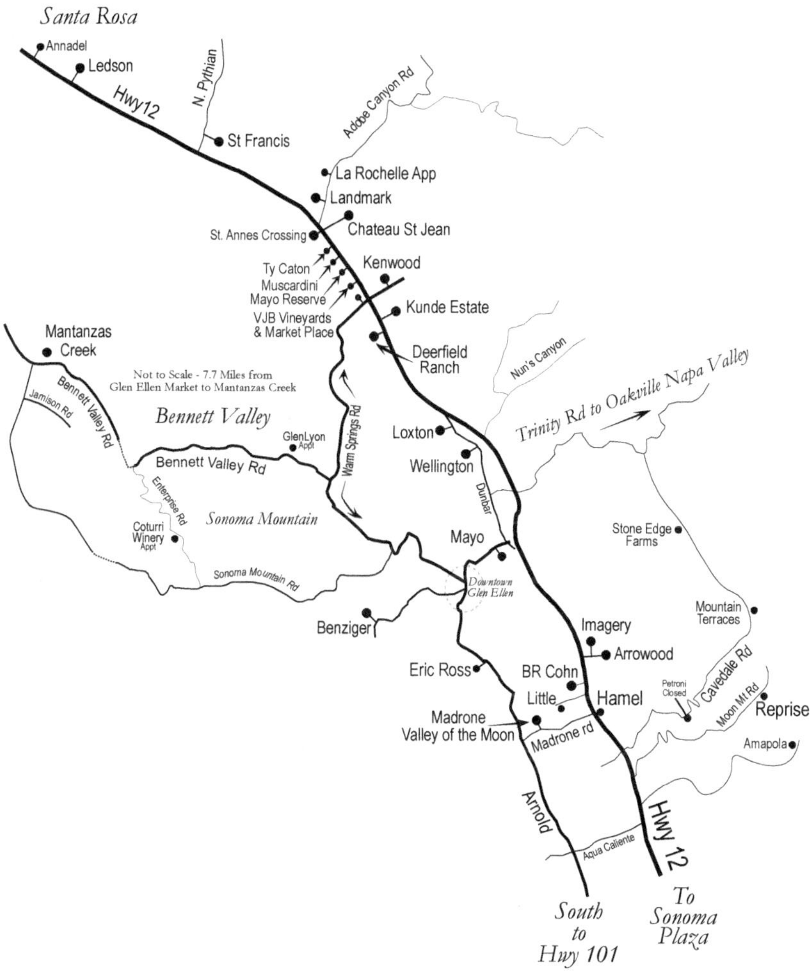

Russian River Valley

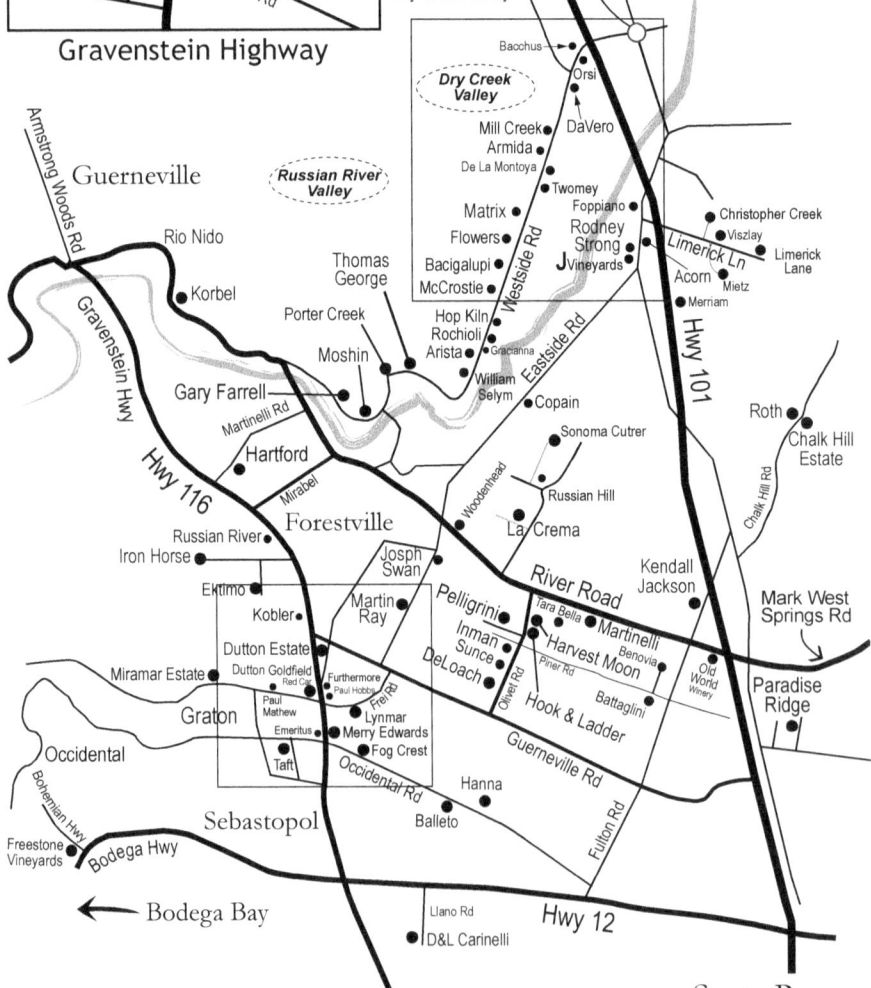

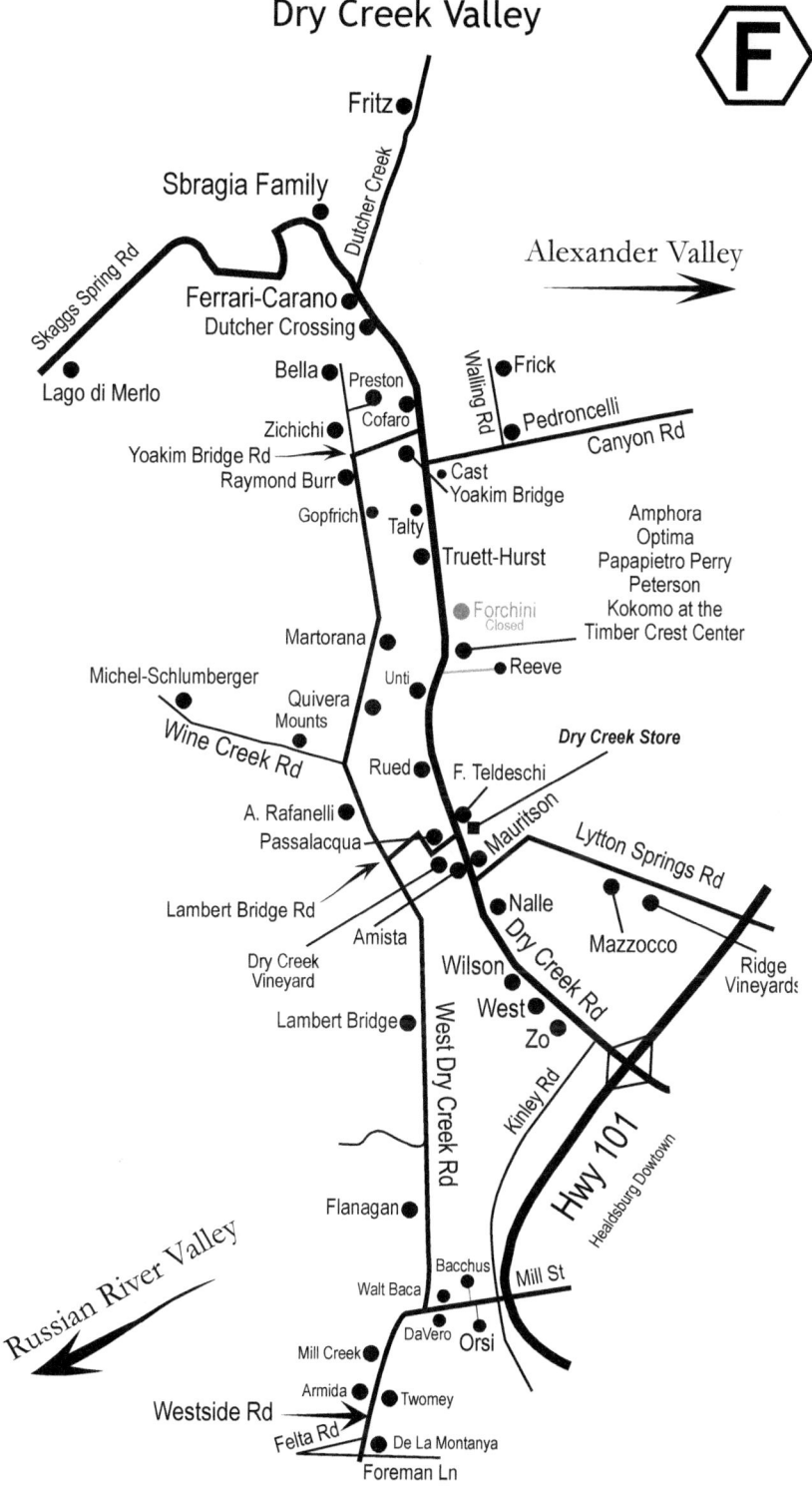

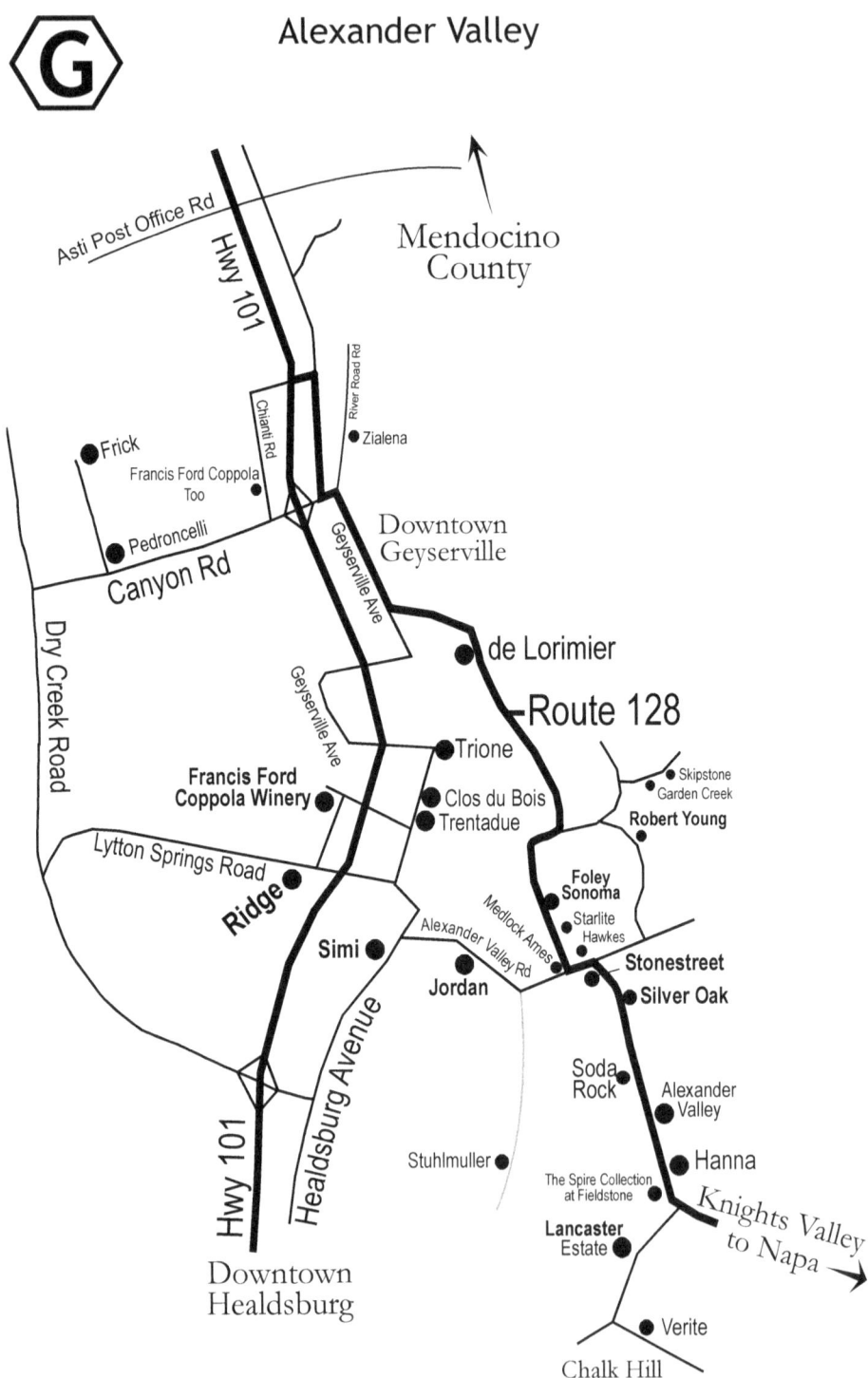

Downtown Healdsburg

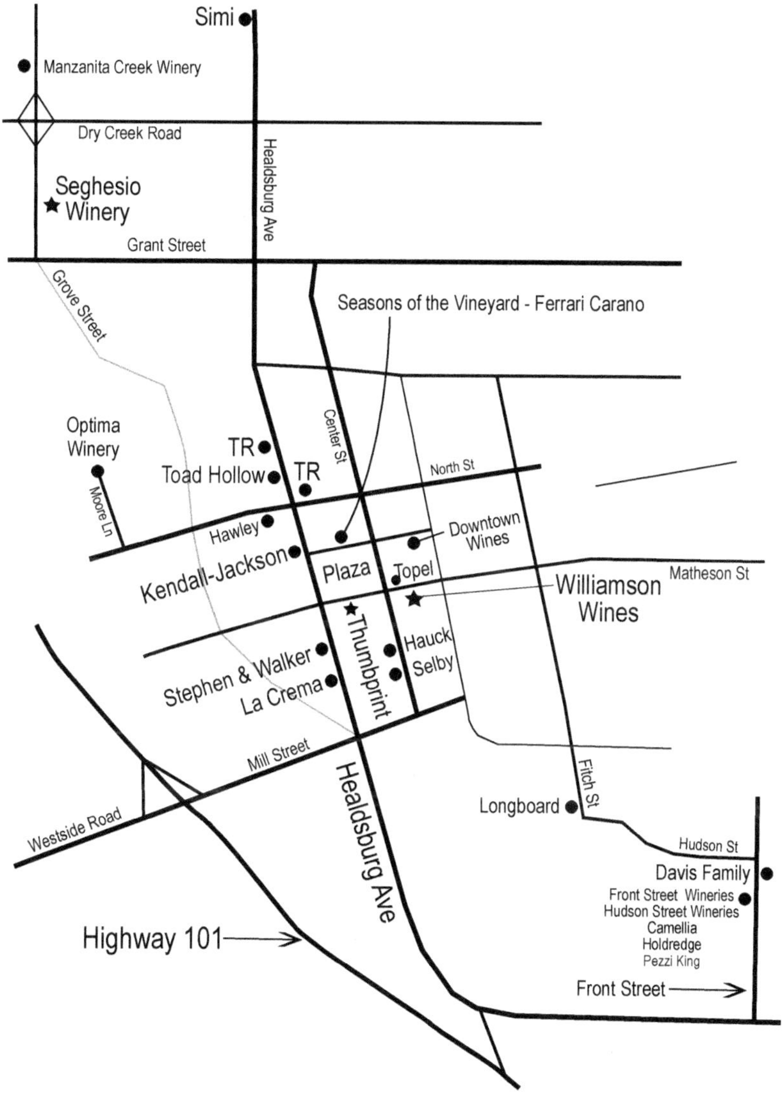

Cuore Libre Publishing
Books and Calendars

WineCountryAtWork.com

A Tour Guide's Napa Valley
A Tour Guide's Sonoma Wine Country
Wine Country in Shorts, A Tour Guide's Stories

Watch the Author's TV Show 'Wine Country at Work'

PlanetaryCalendar.com
Published Annually since 1949

Planetary Calendar Astrology Forecasts & Health Hints
Two Wall Sizes, a Pocket Size, a Day Planner &
a Digital Version for your Phone and Computer

The Companion Book
'Planetary Calendar Astrology,
Moving Beyond Observation to Action'

Watch the Author's Weekly Forecasts & Astro Portraits

SpaceAndTime.com

From the 'Tango' Series
Feng Shui and the Tango, The Dance of Design
Prosperity Lessons
Happiness Lessons
The Dream Desk Quiz
Creating Clarity

From the '10 Minute' Series
The 10 Minute Herbalist
Good Health is Easy, It's Being Sick That's Rough
A Year of Healthful Hints